50 MANDALAS

Volume 1

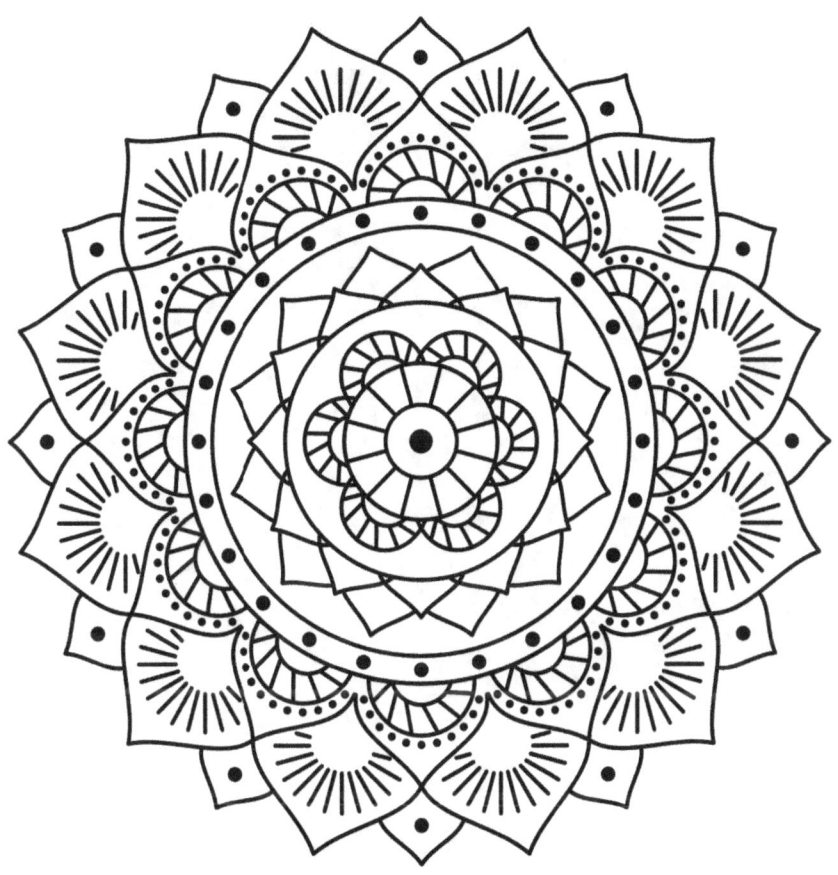

A Coloring Book for Adults Featuring 50
Beautiful and Unique Mandalas for Stress
Relief and Relaxation.

This Book
Belongs To :

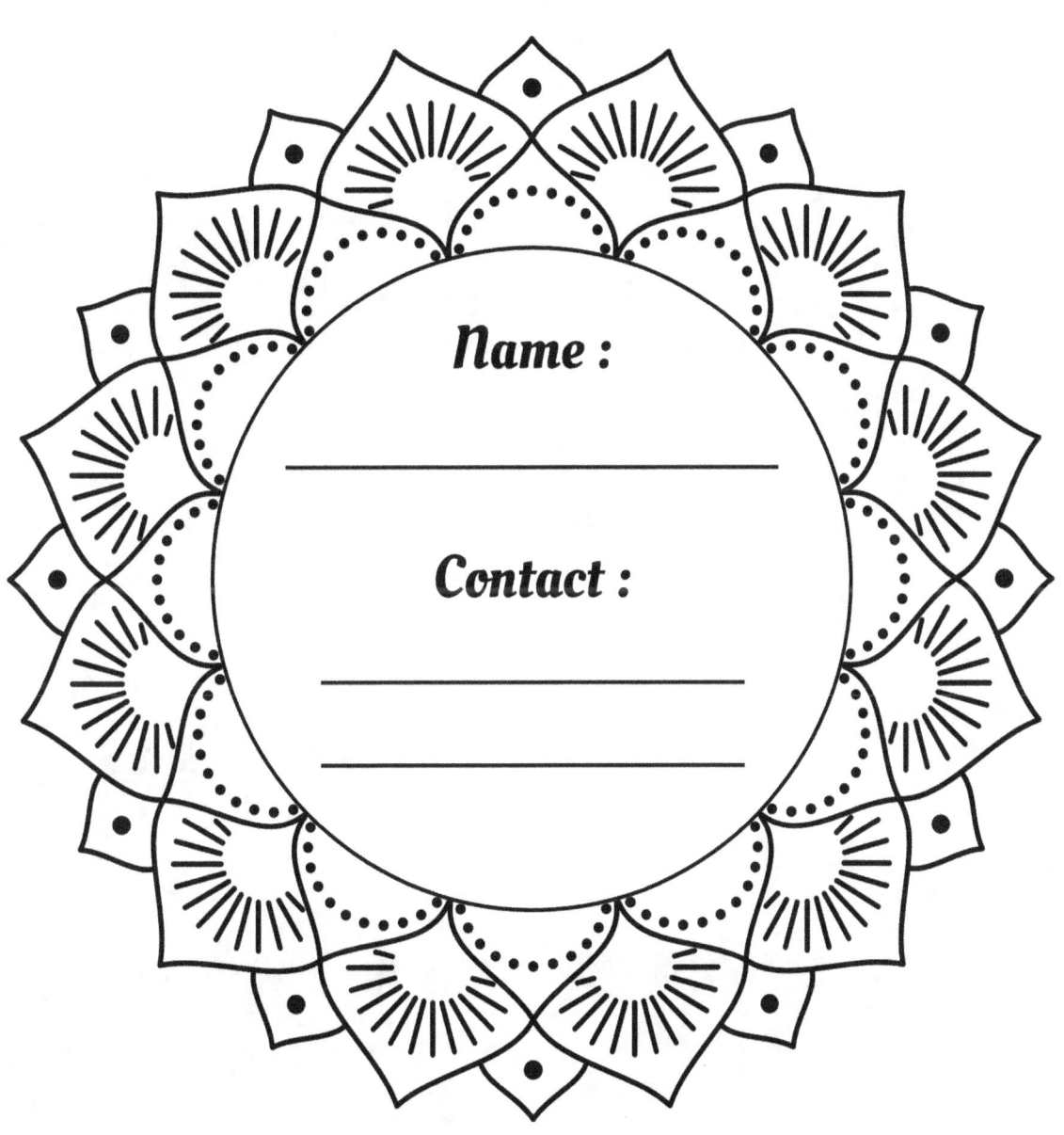

Name :

_____

Contact :

_____

Color Test Page

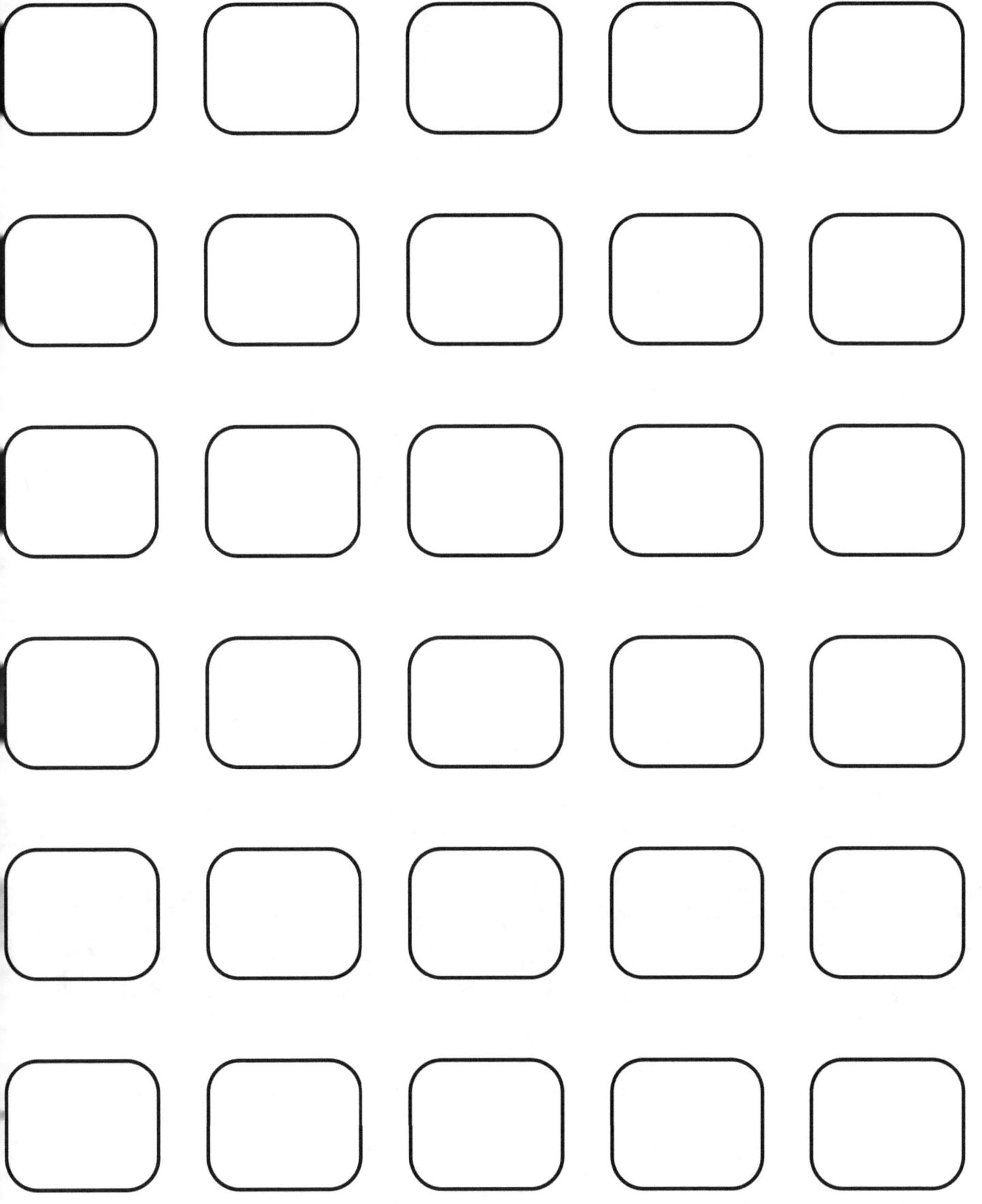

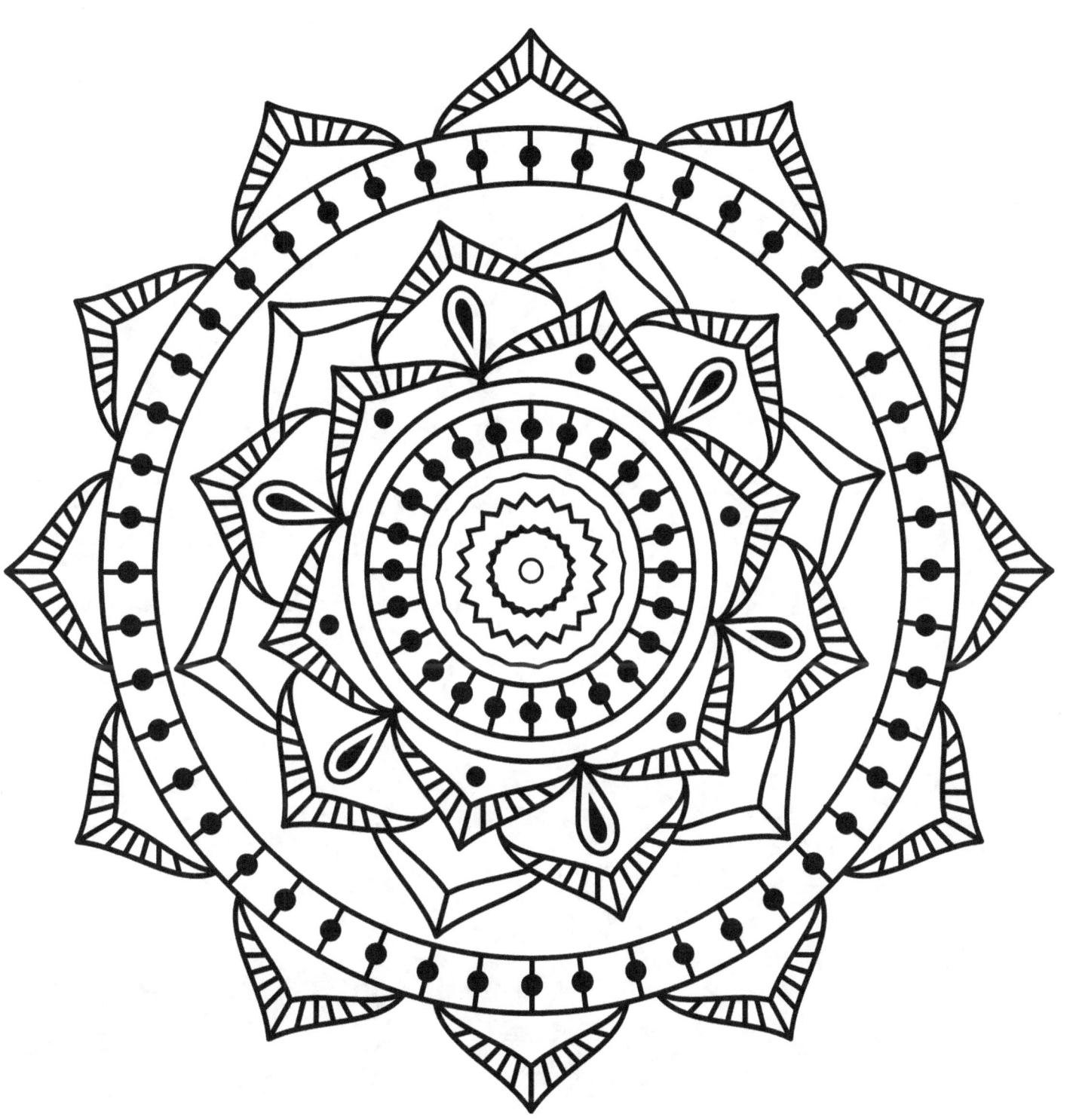

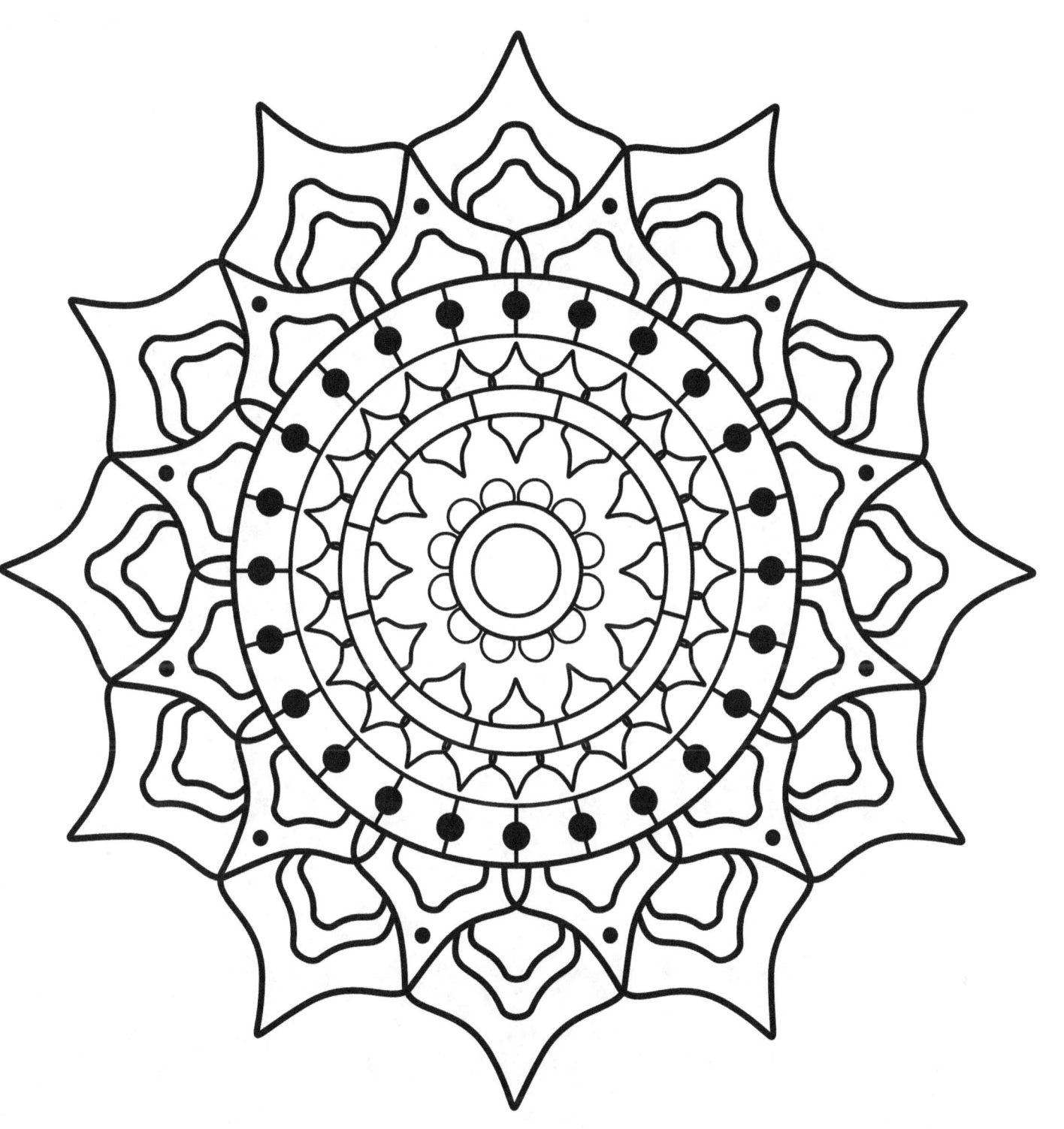

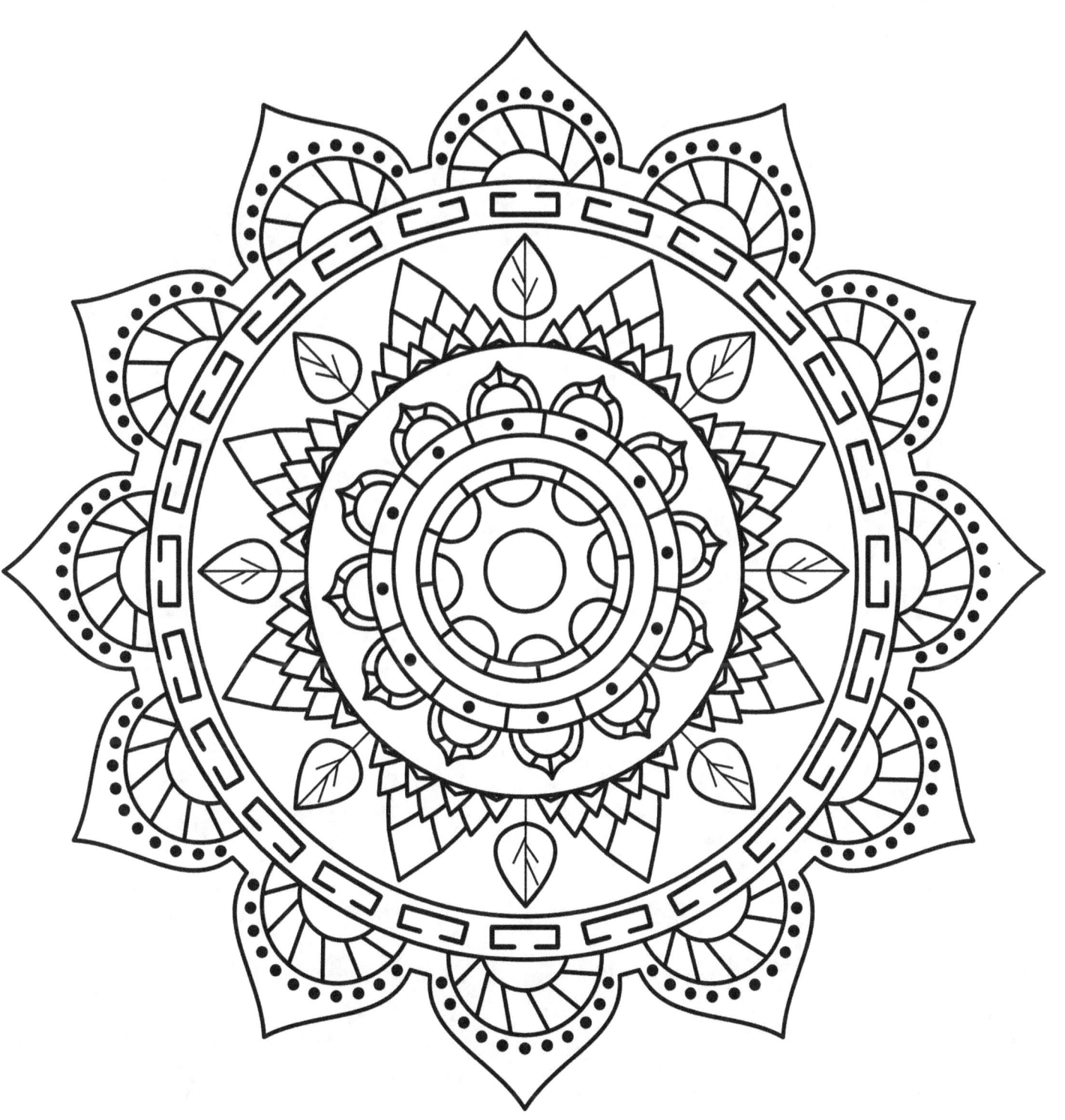

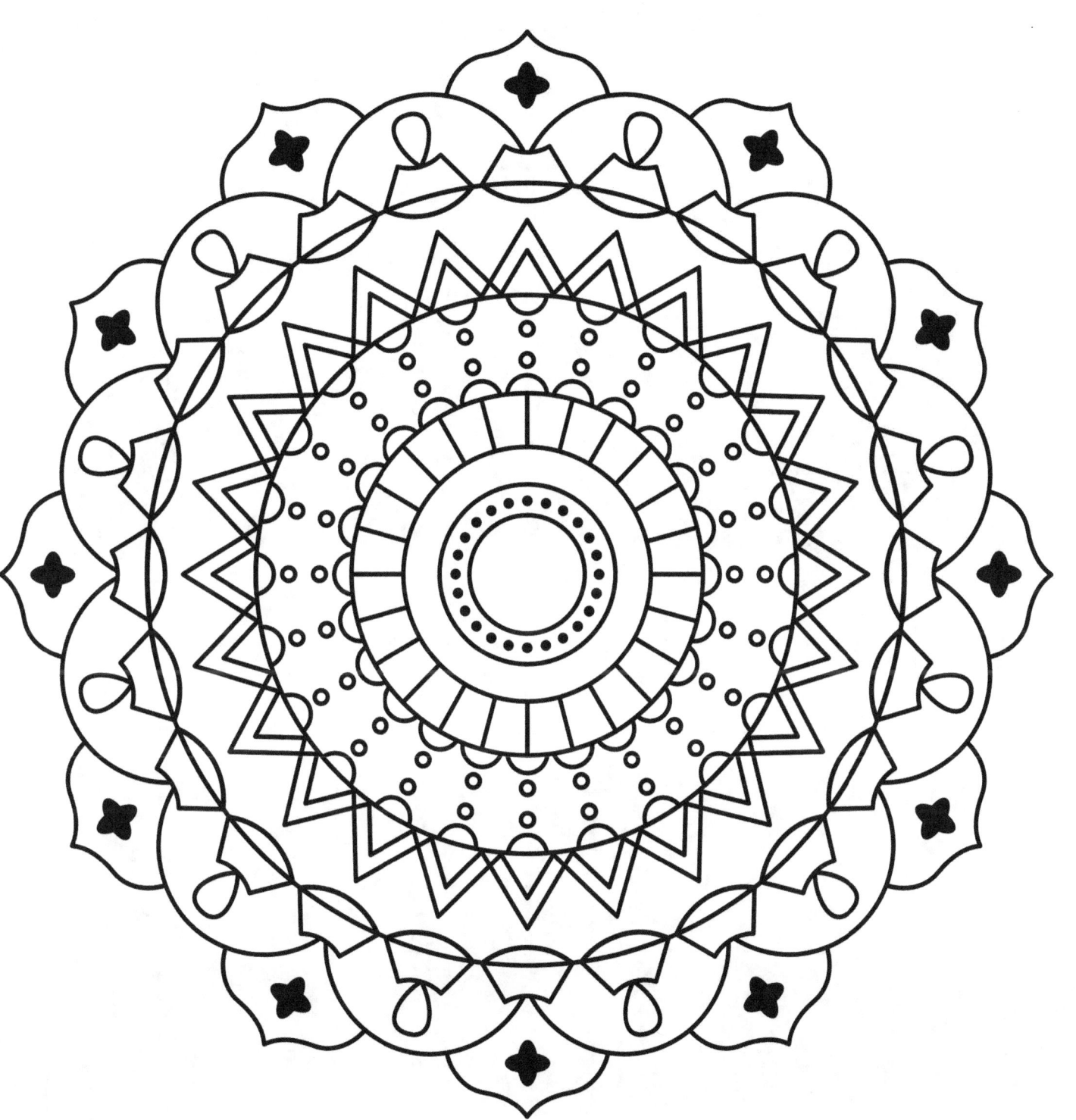

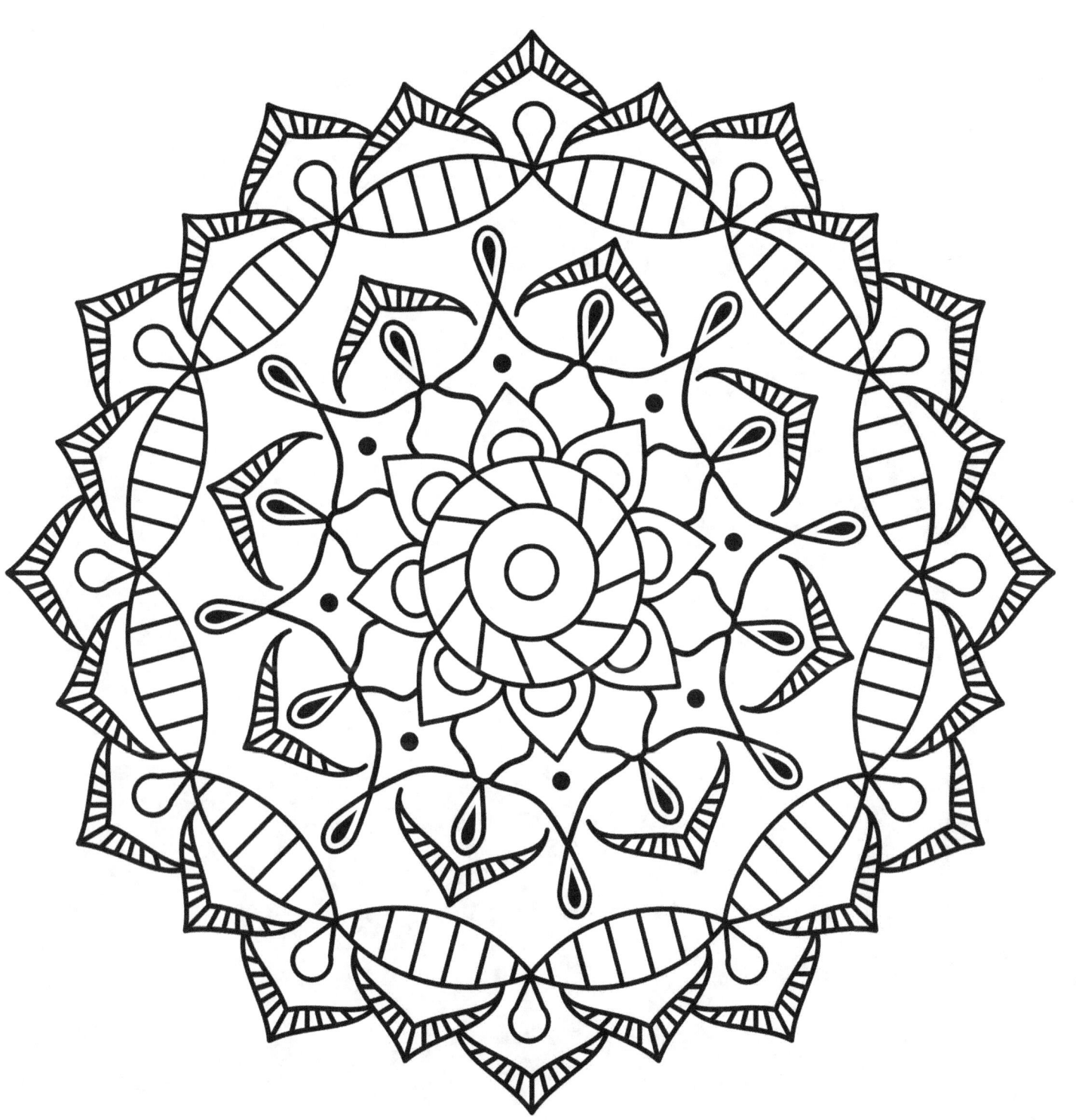

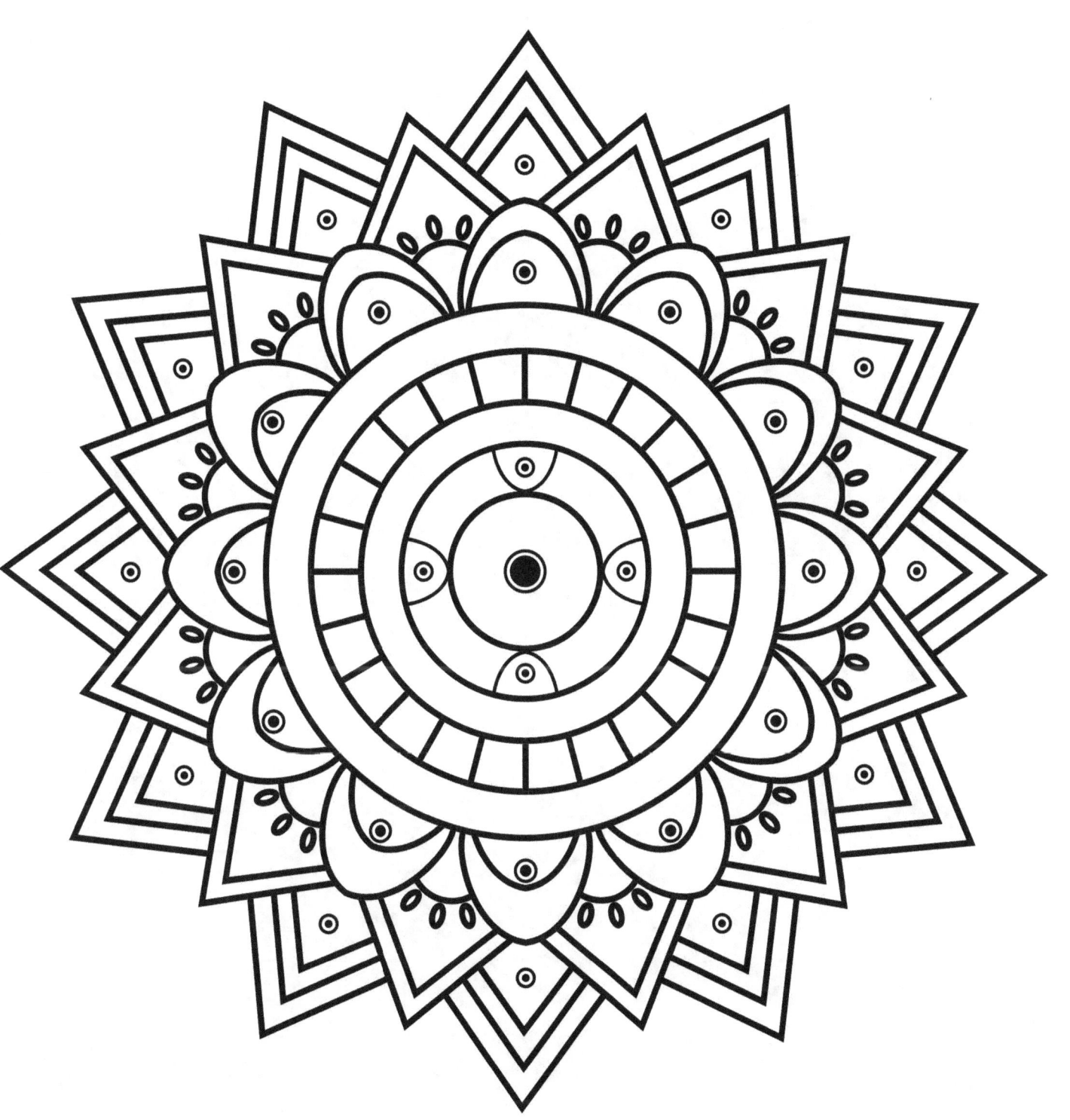

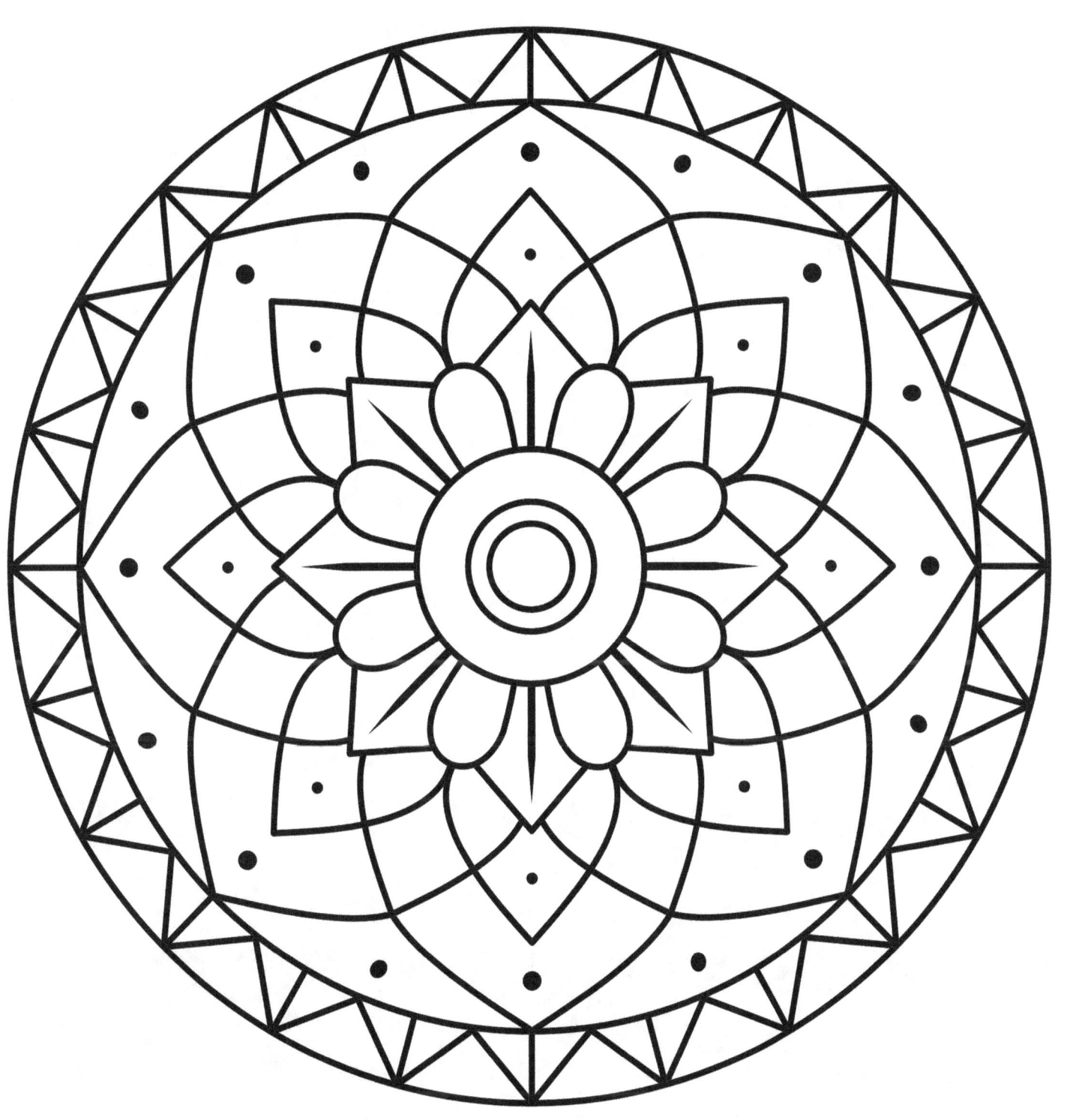

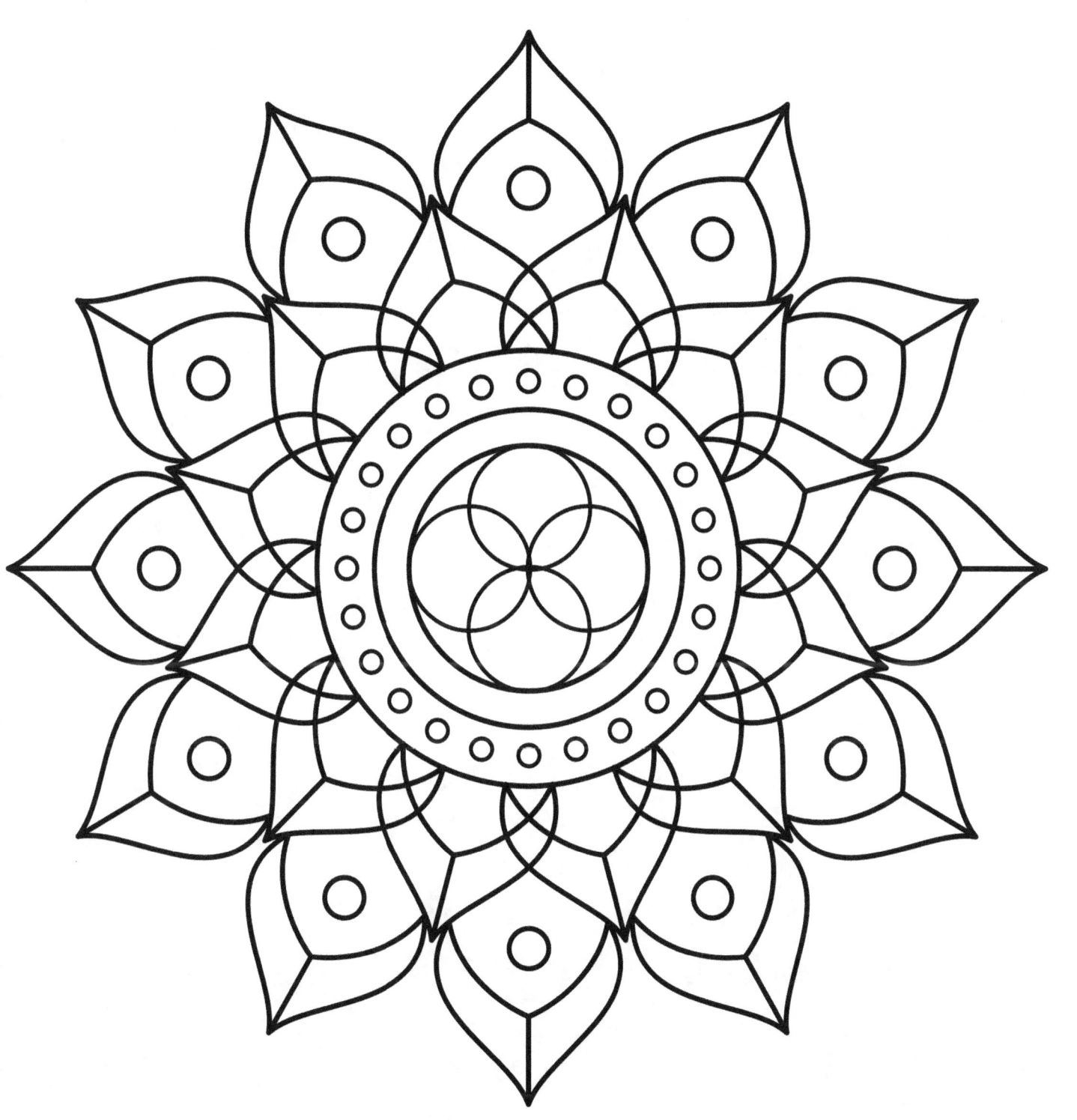

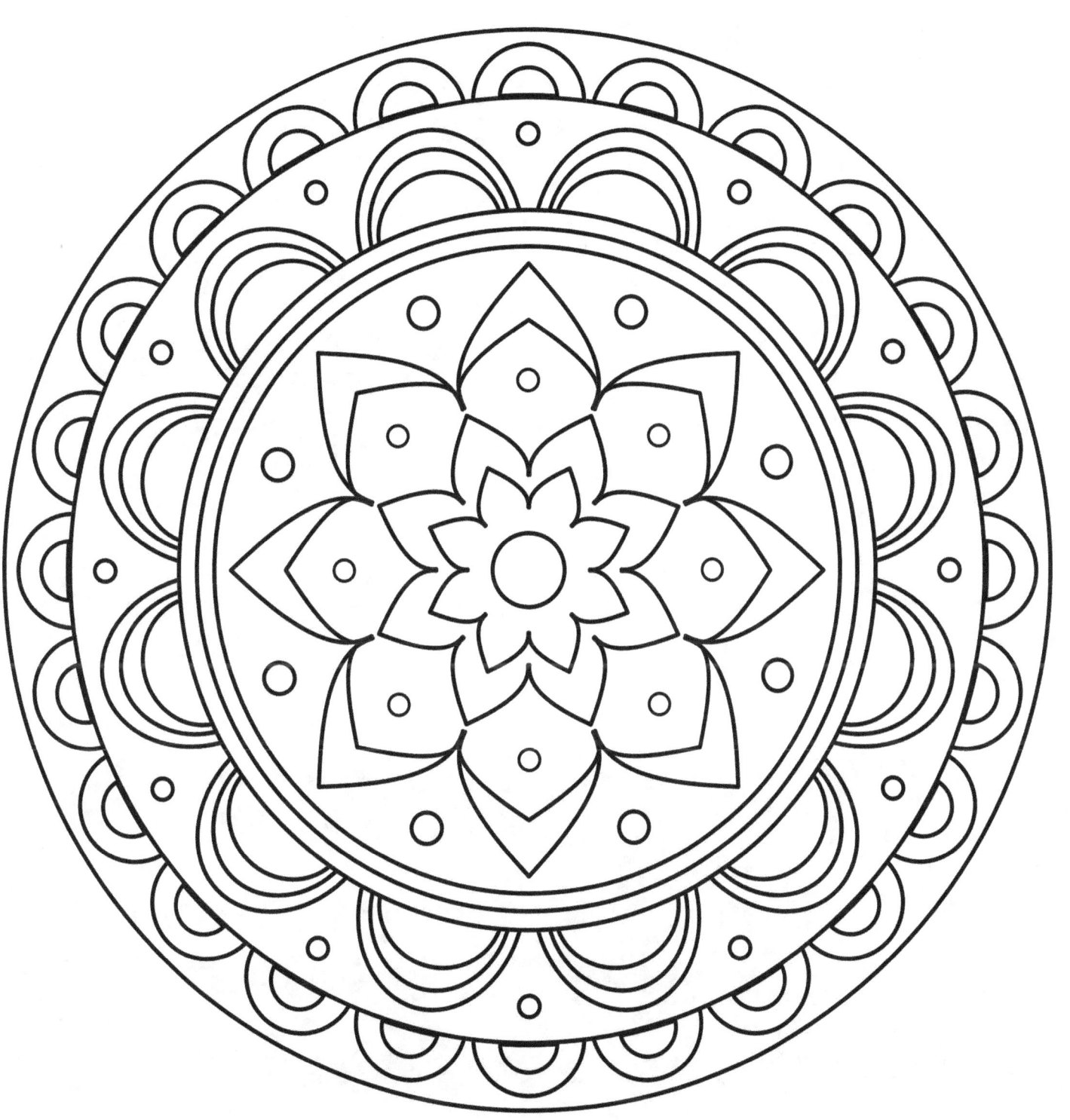

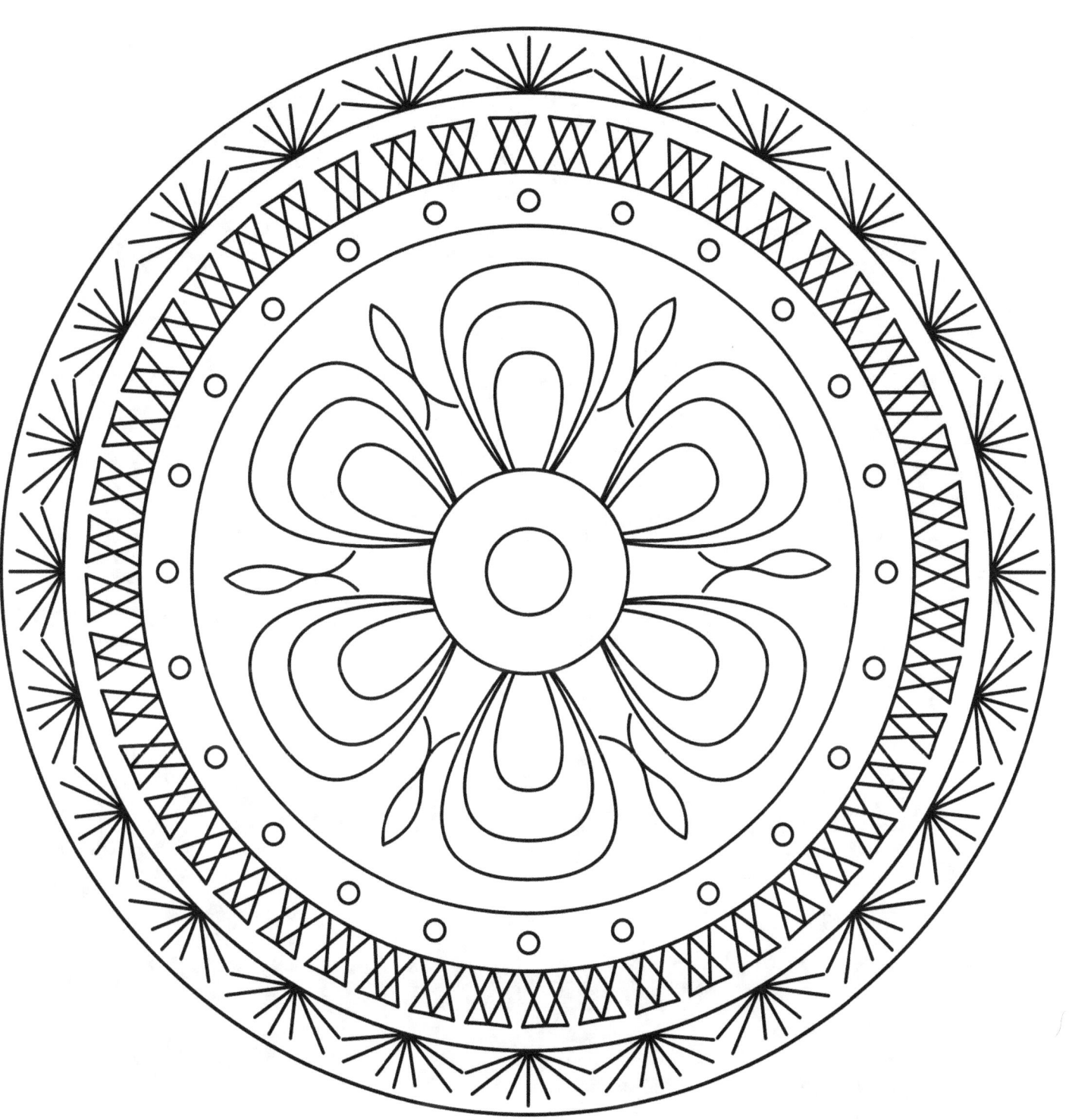

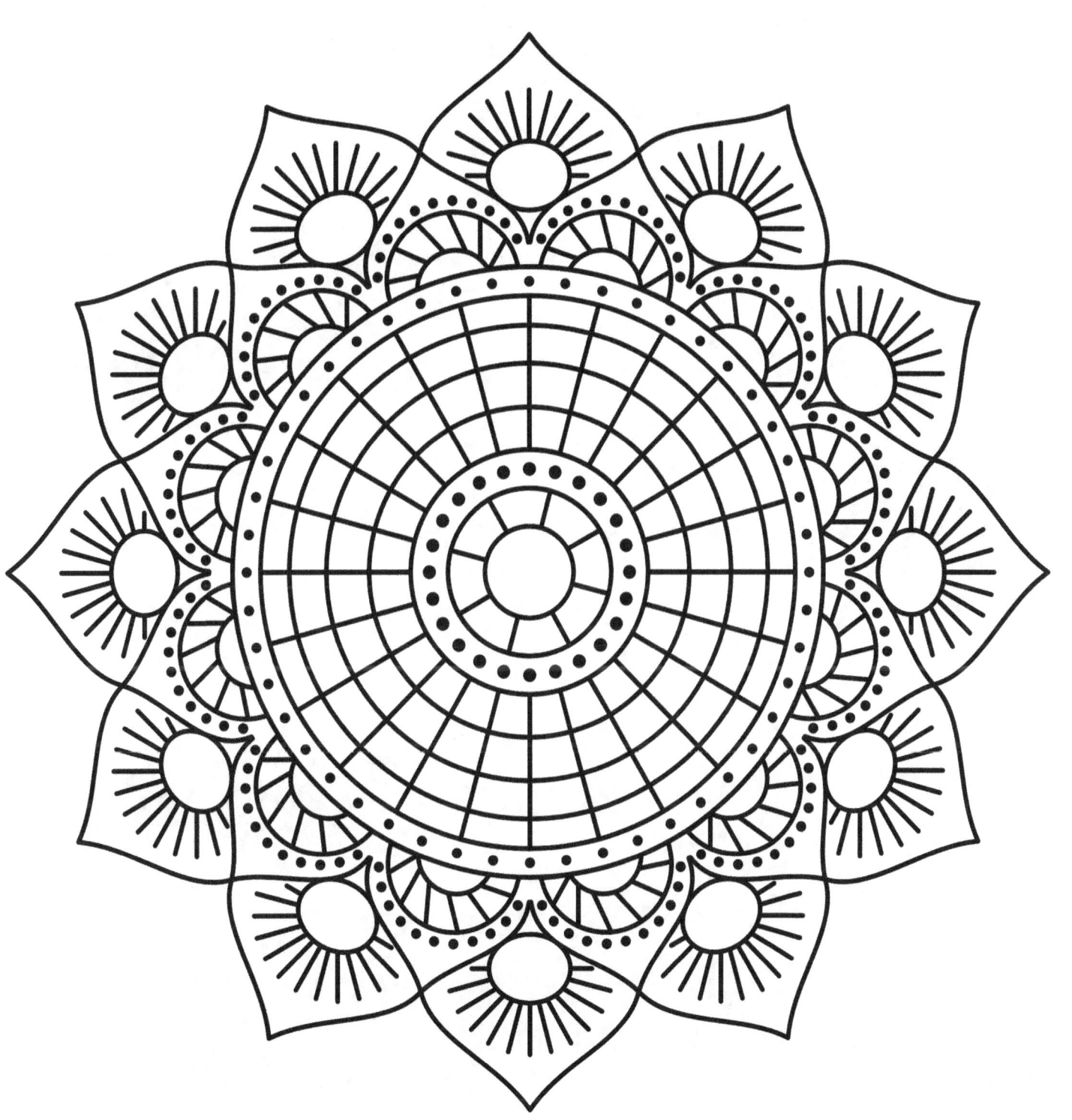

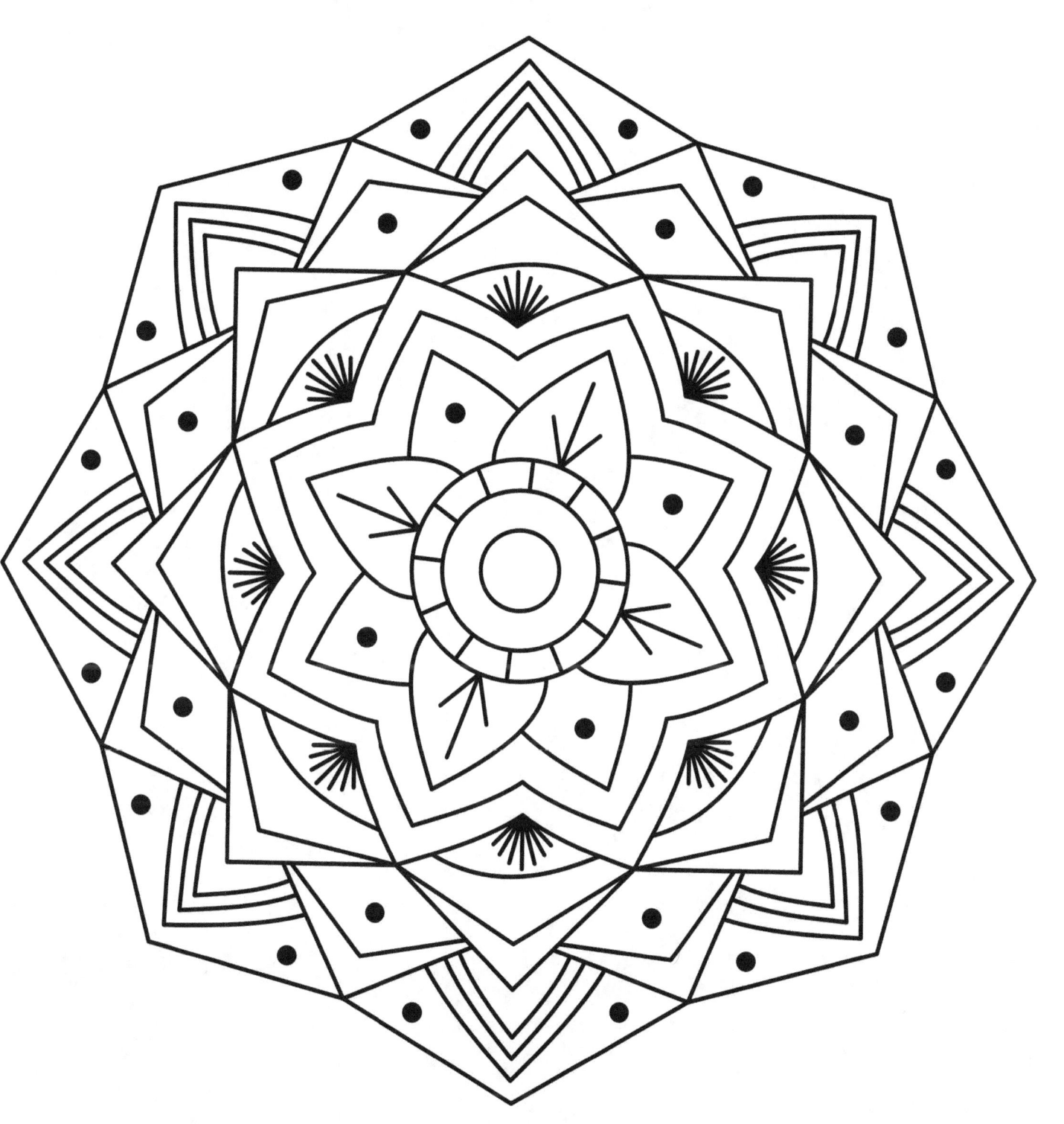

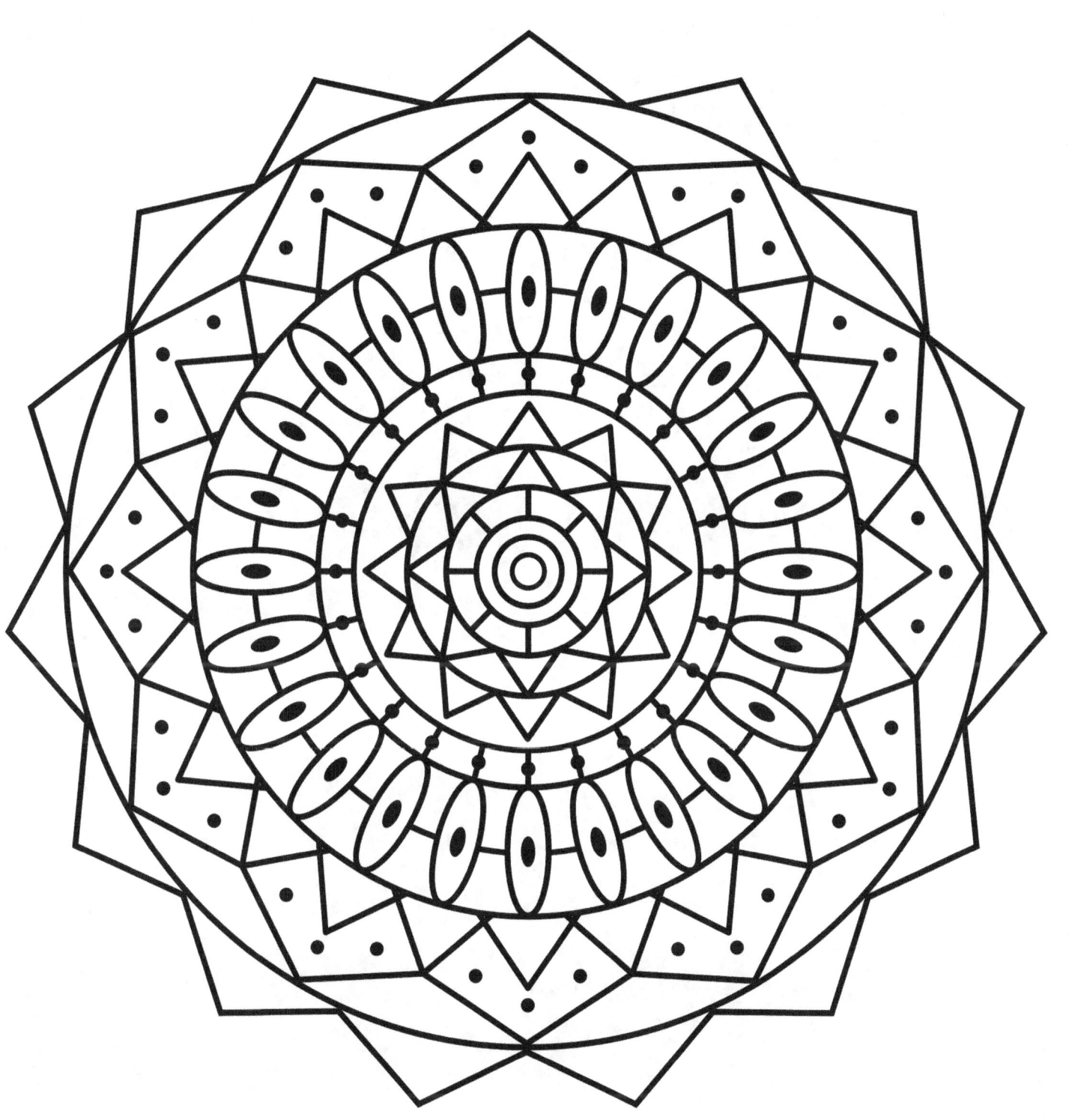

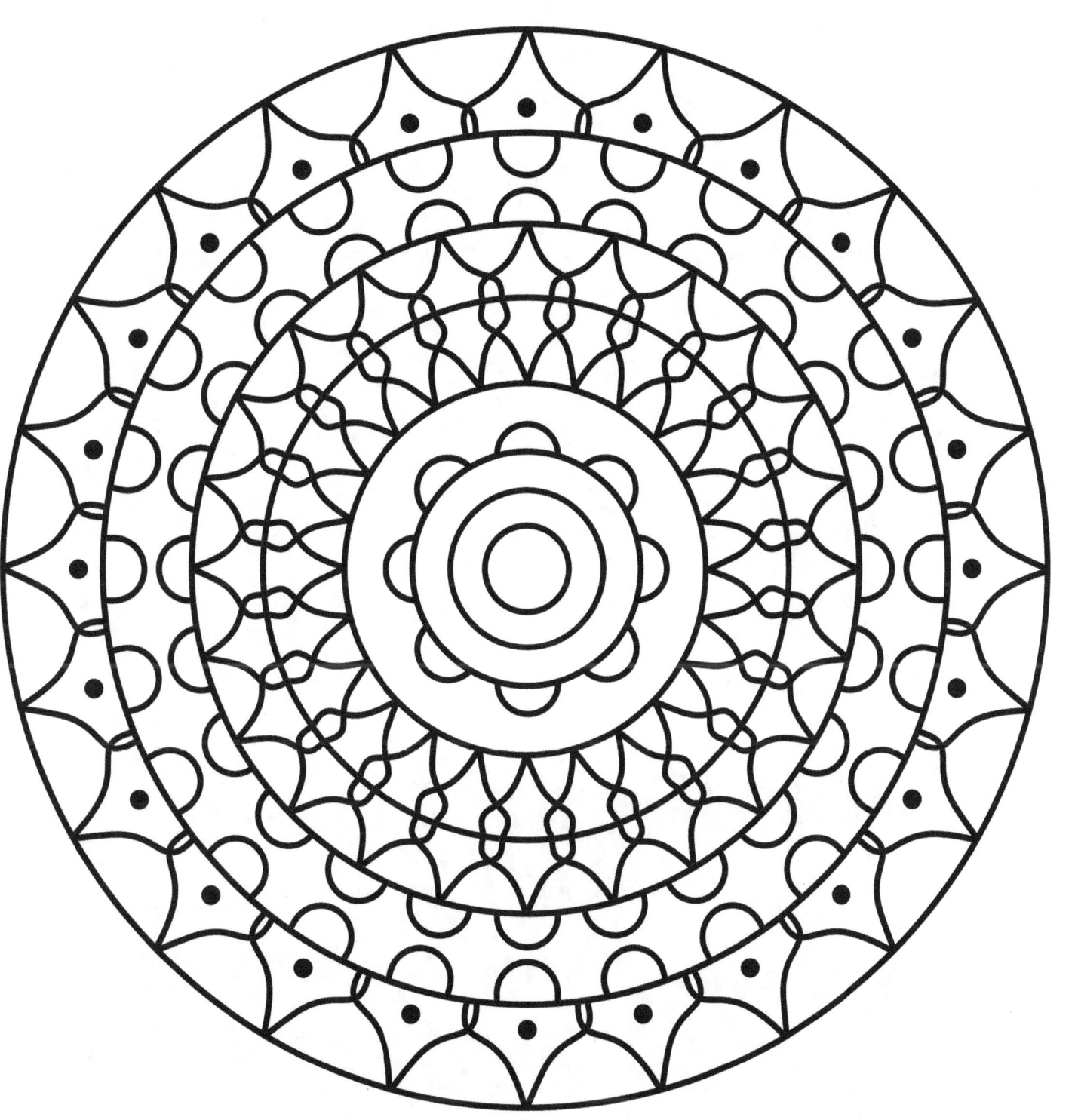

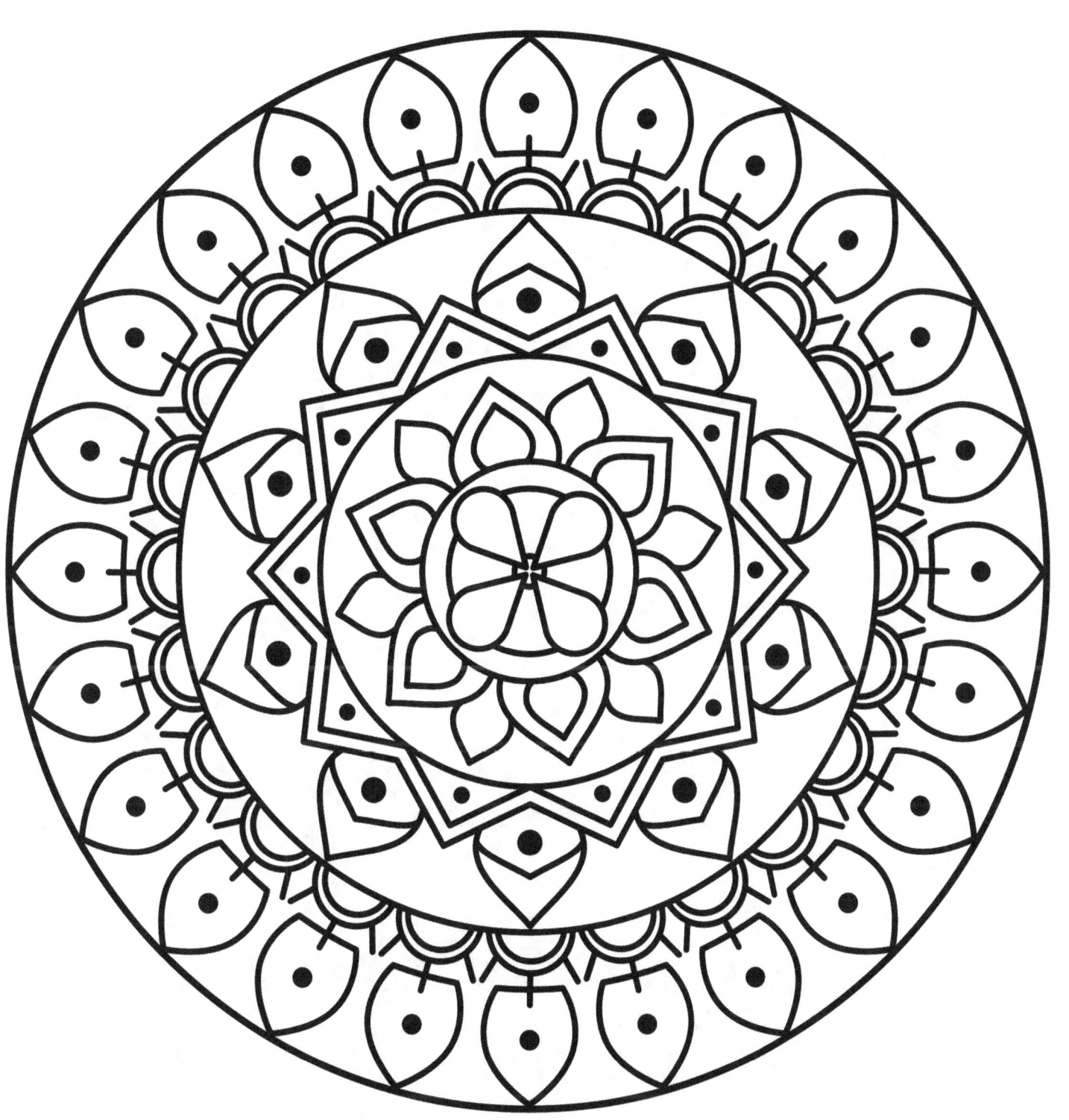

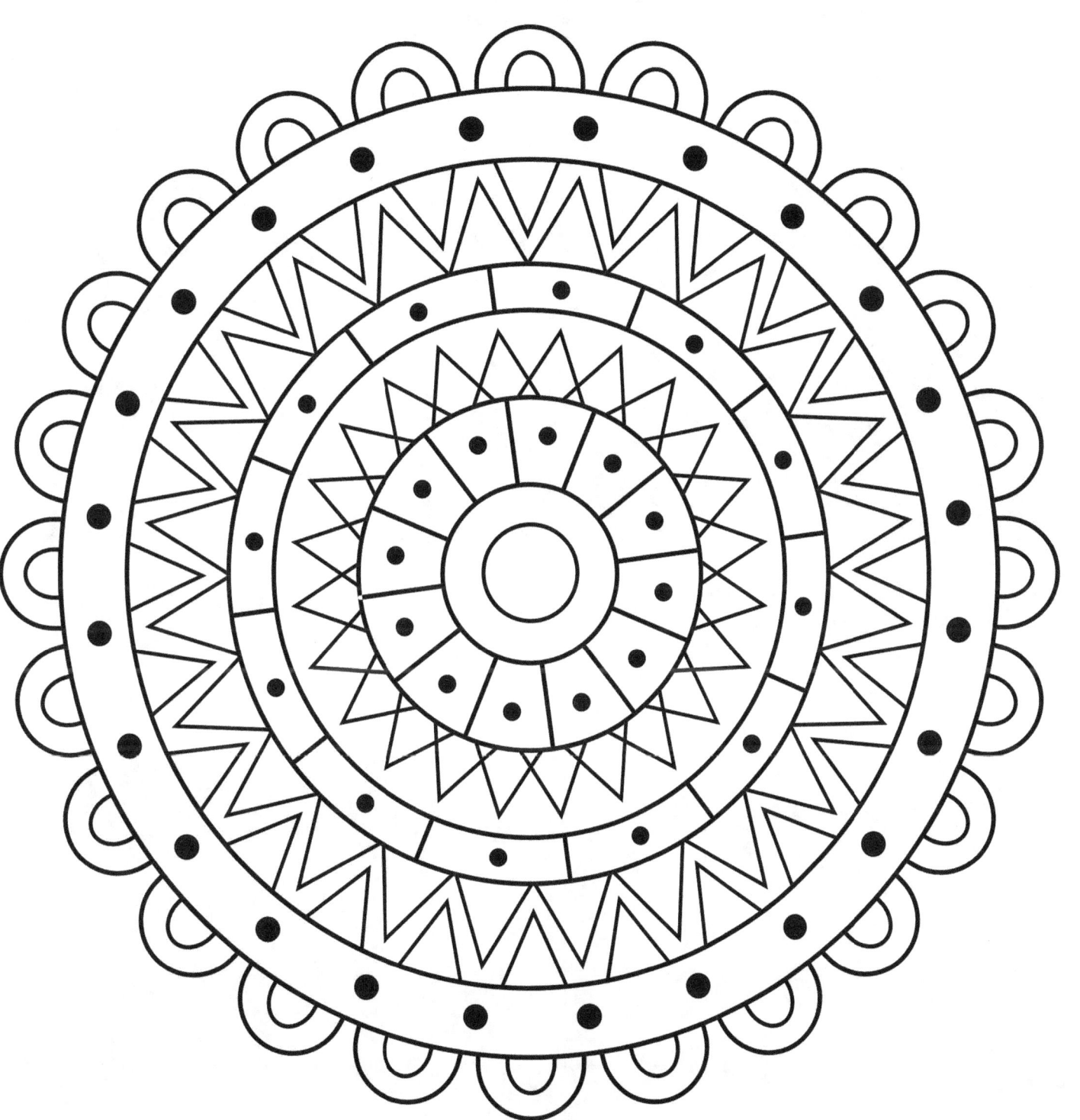

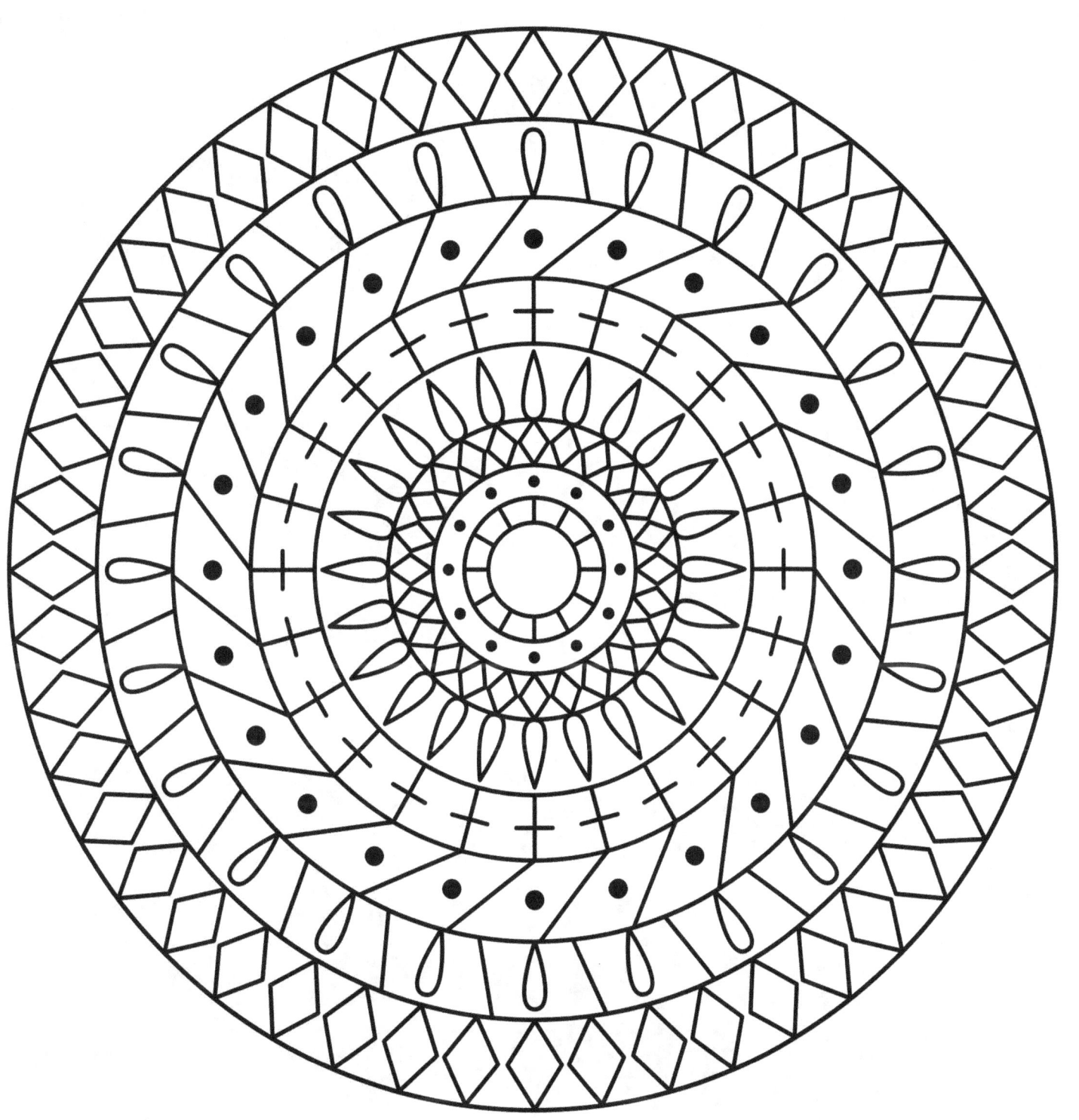

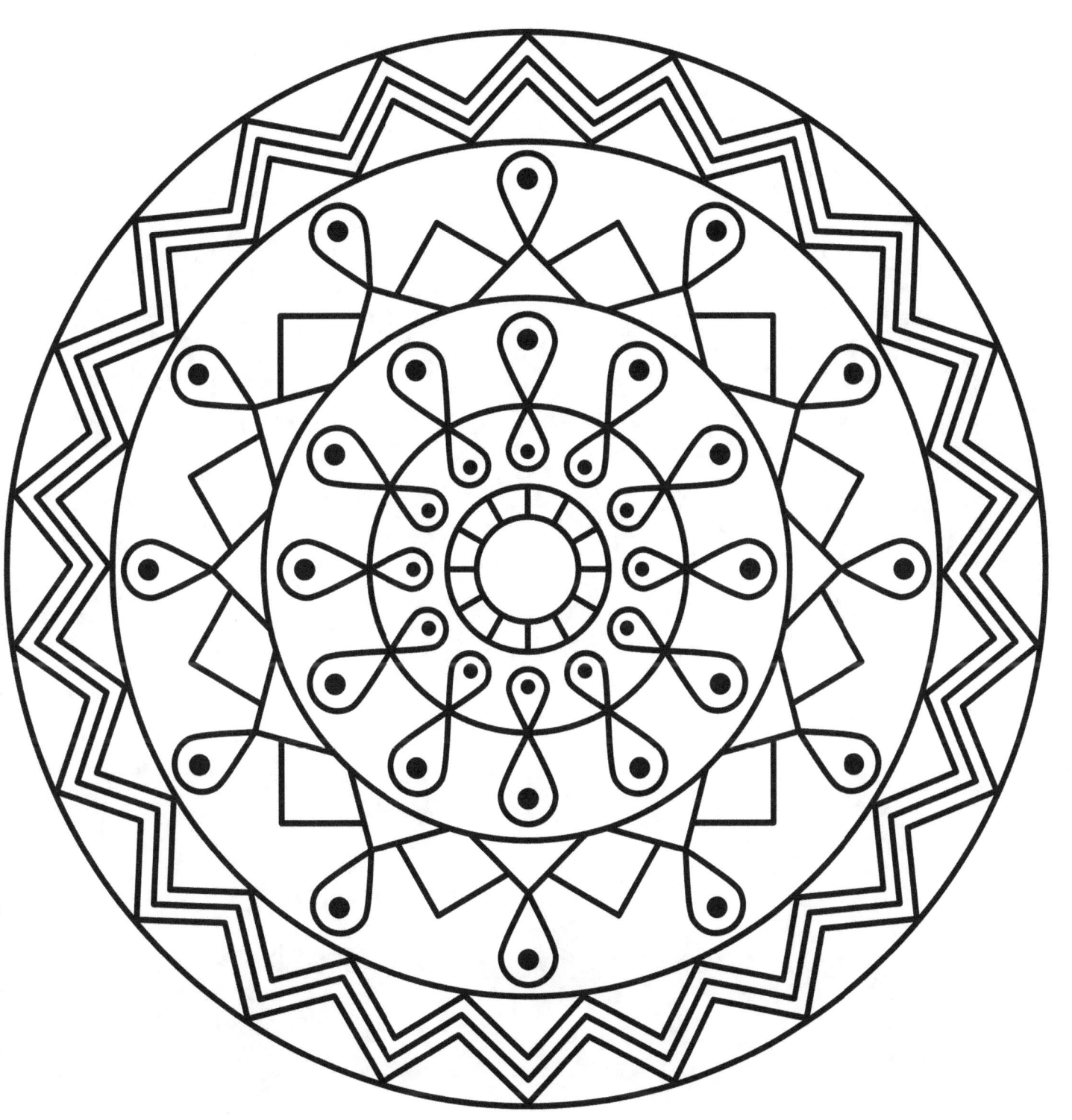

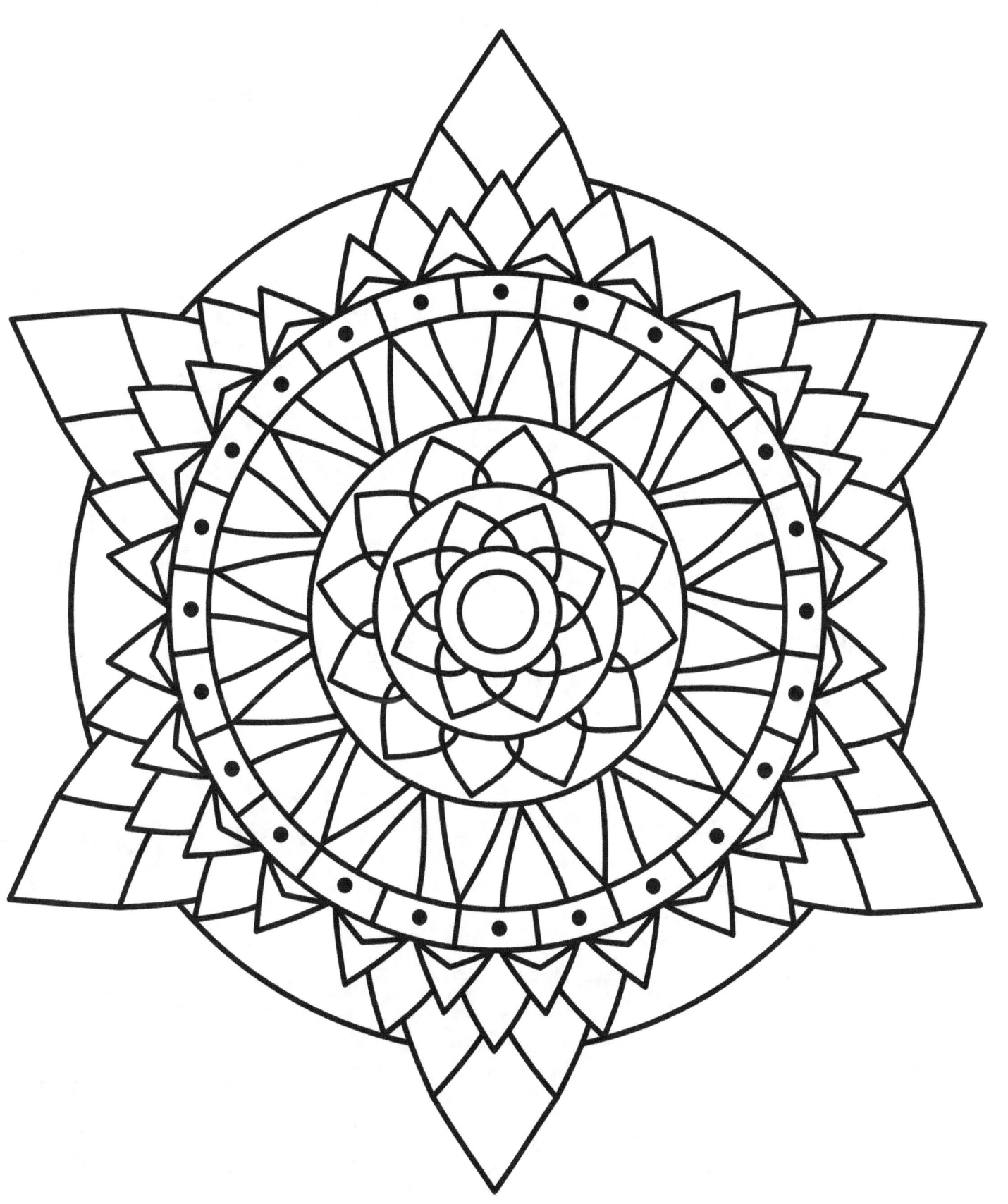

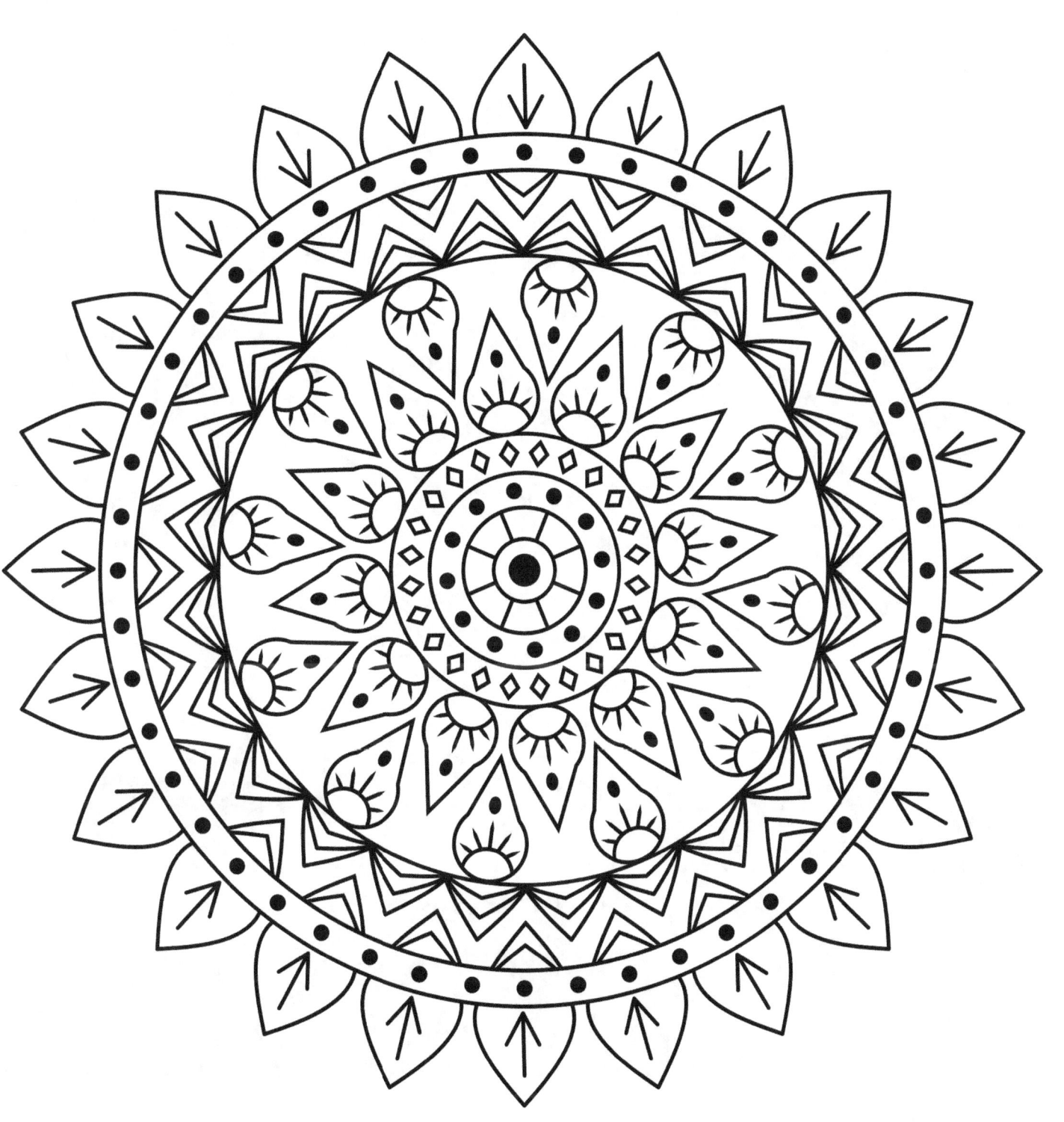

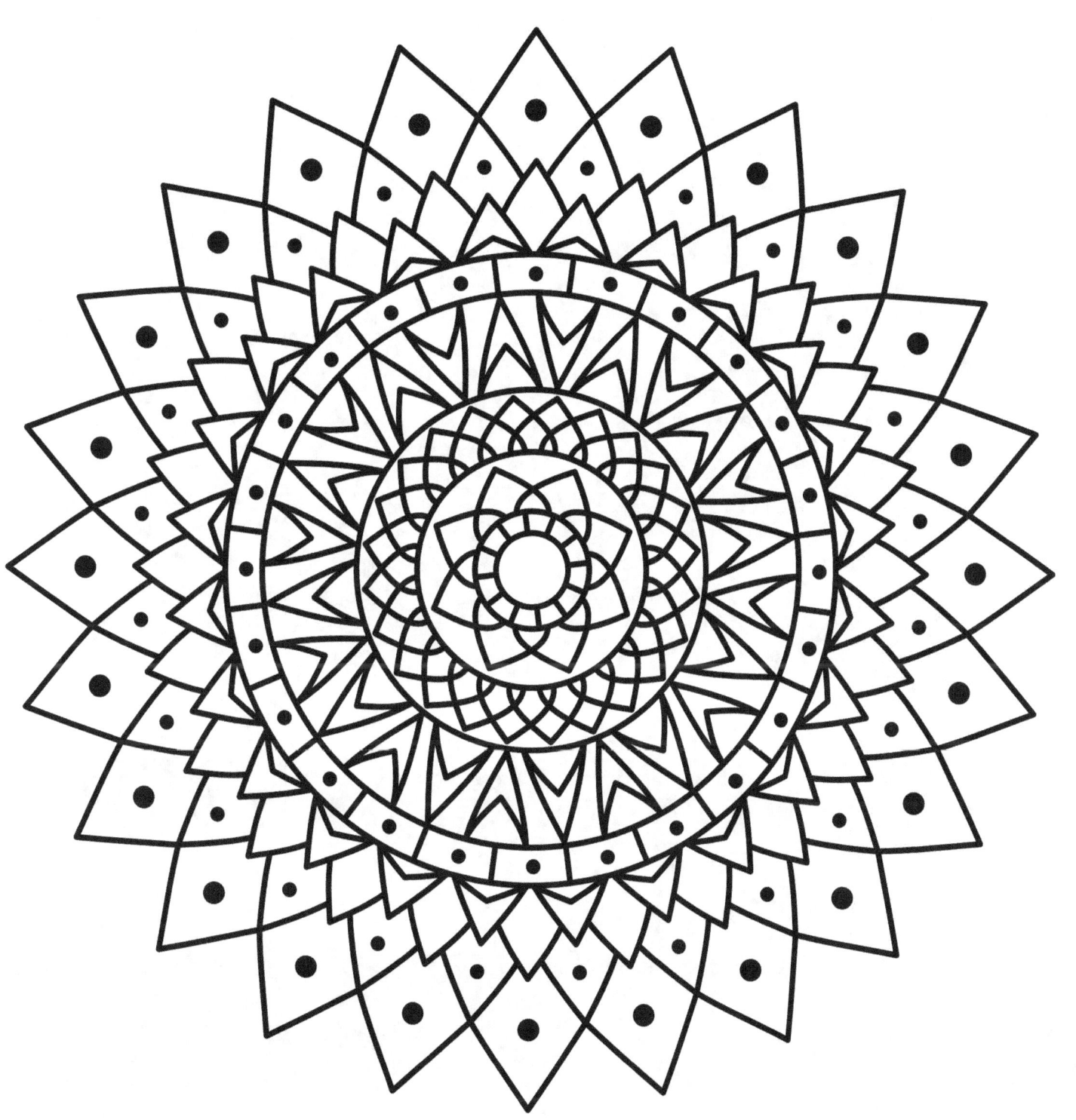

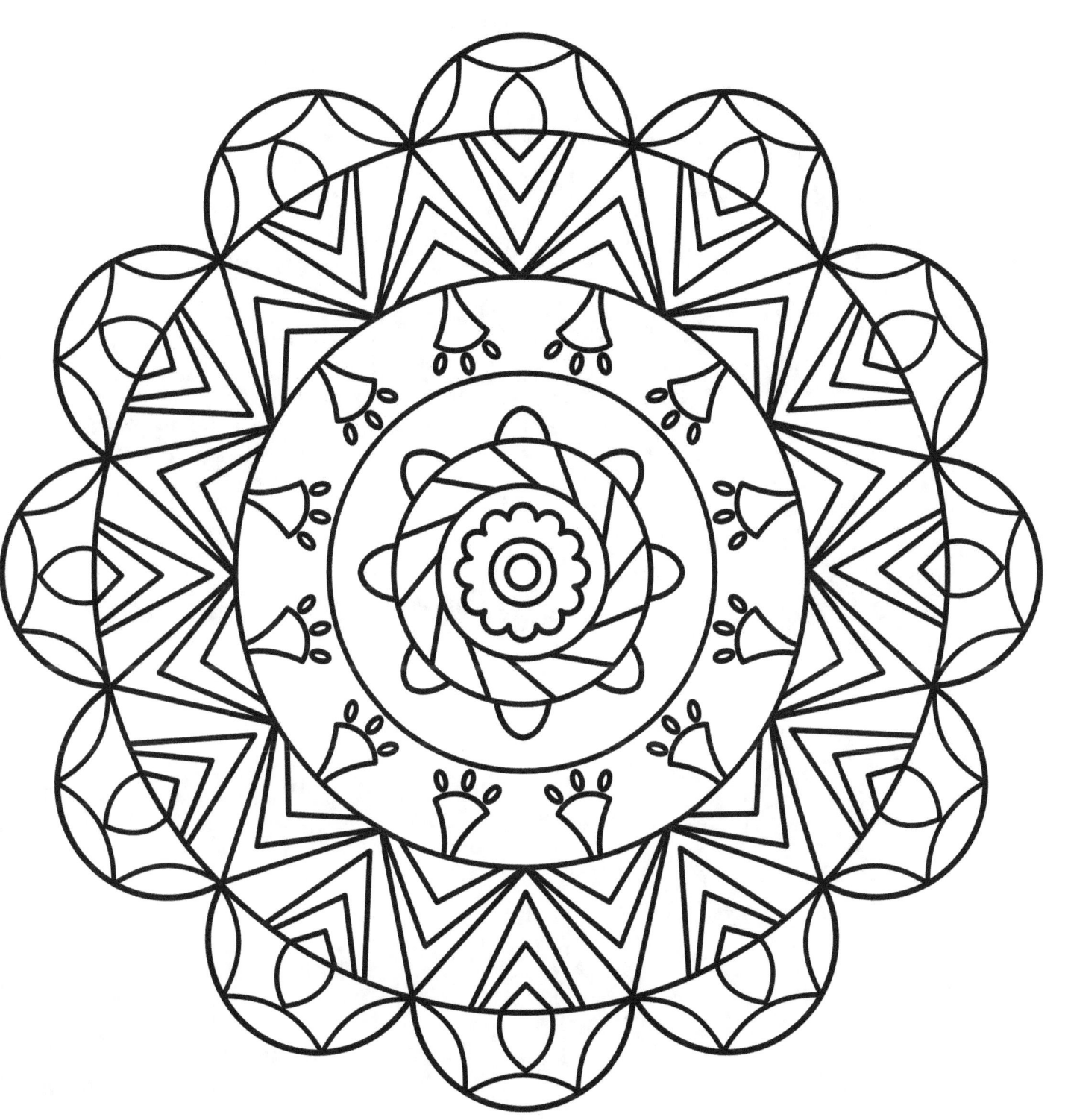

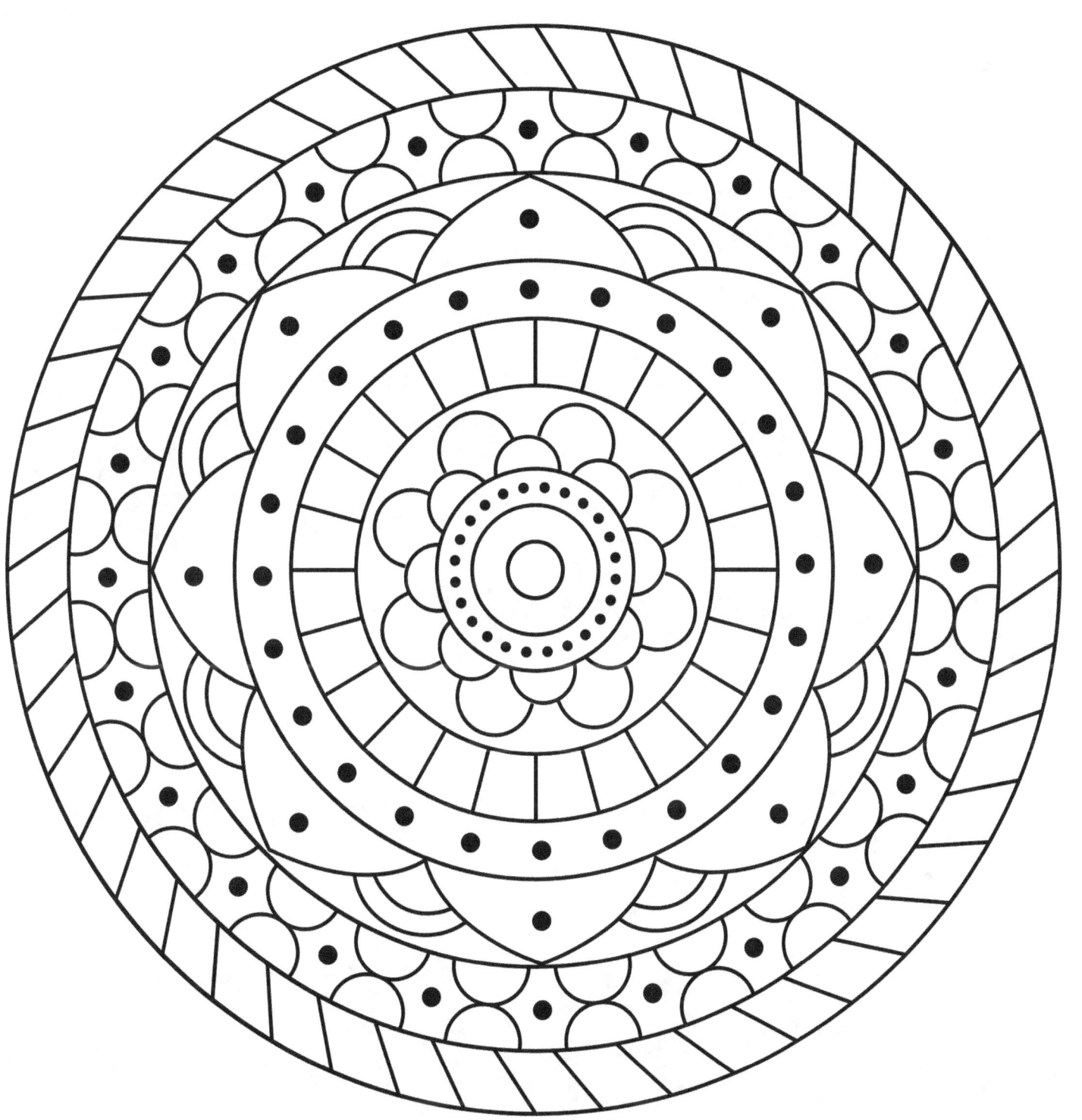

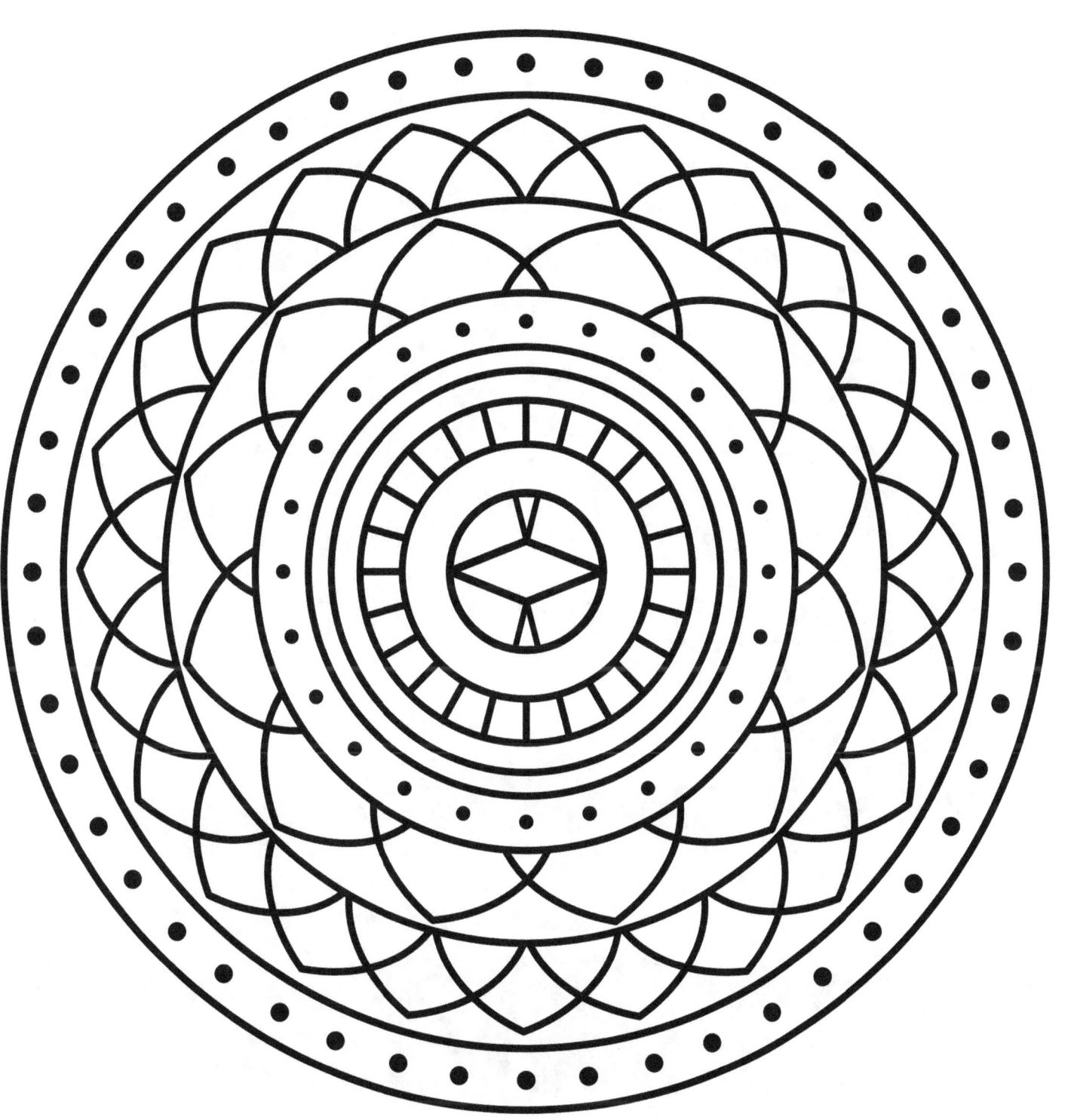

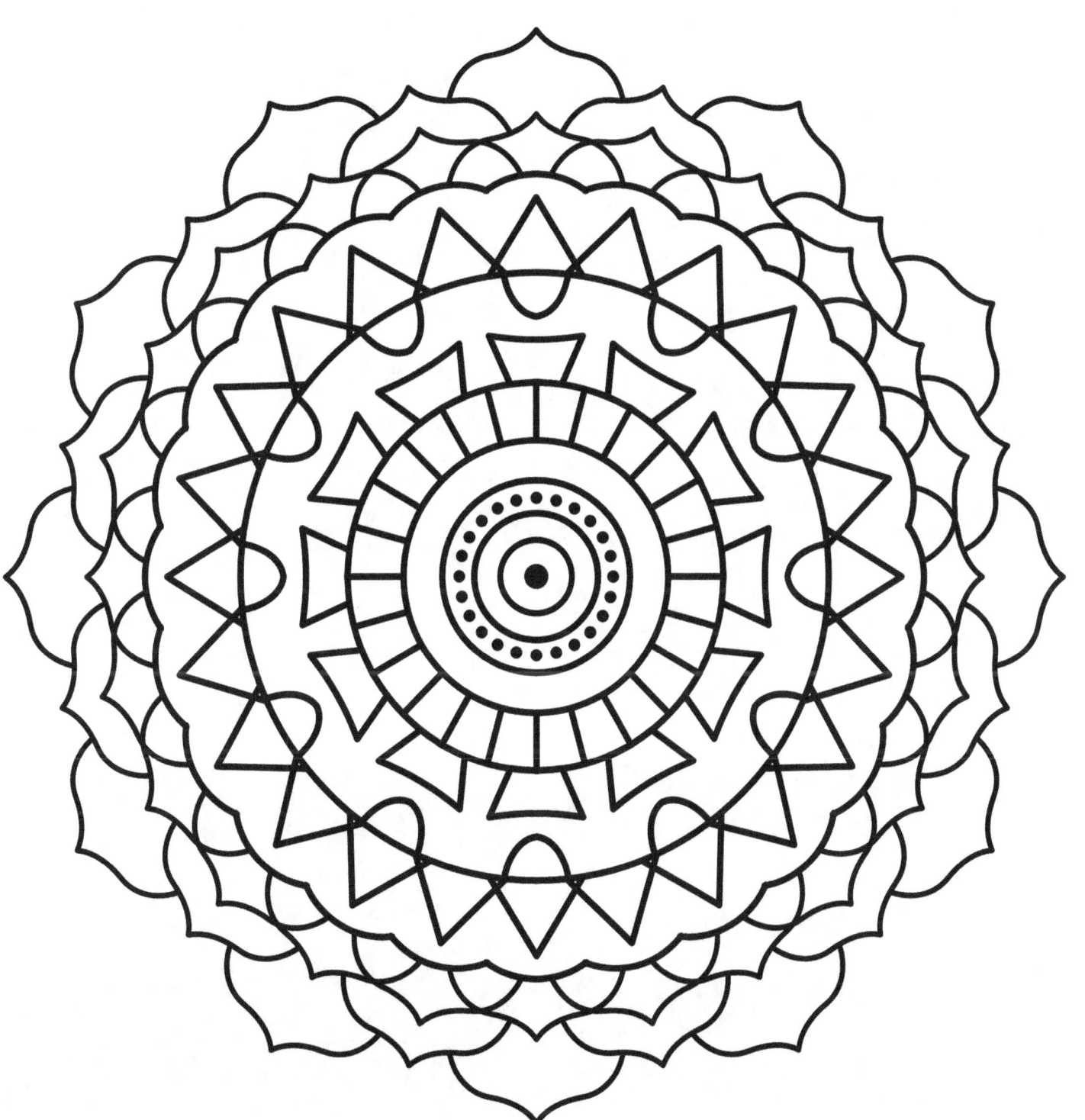

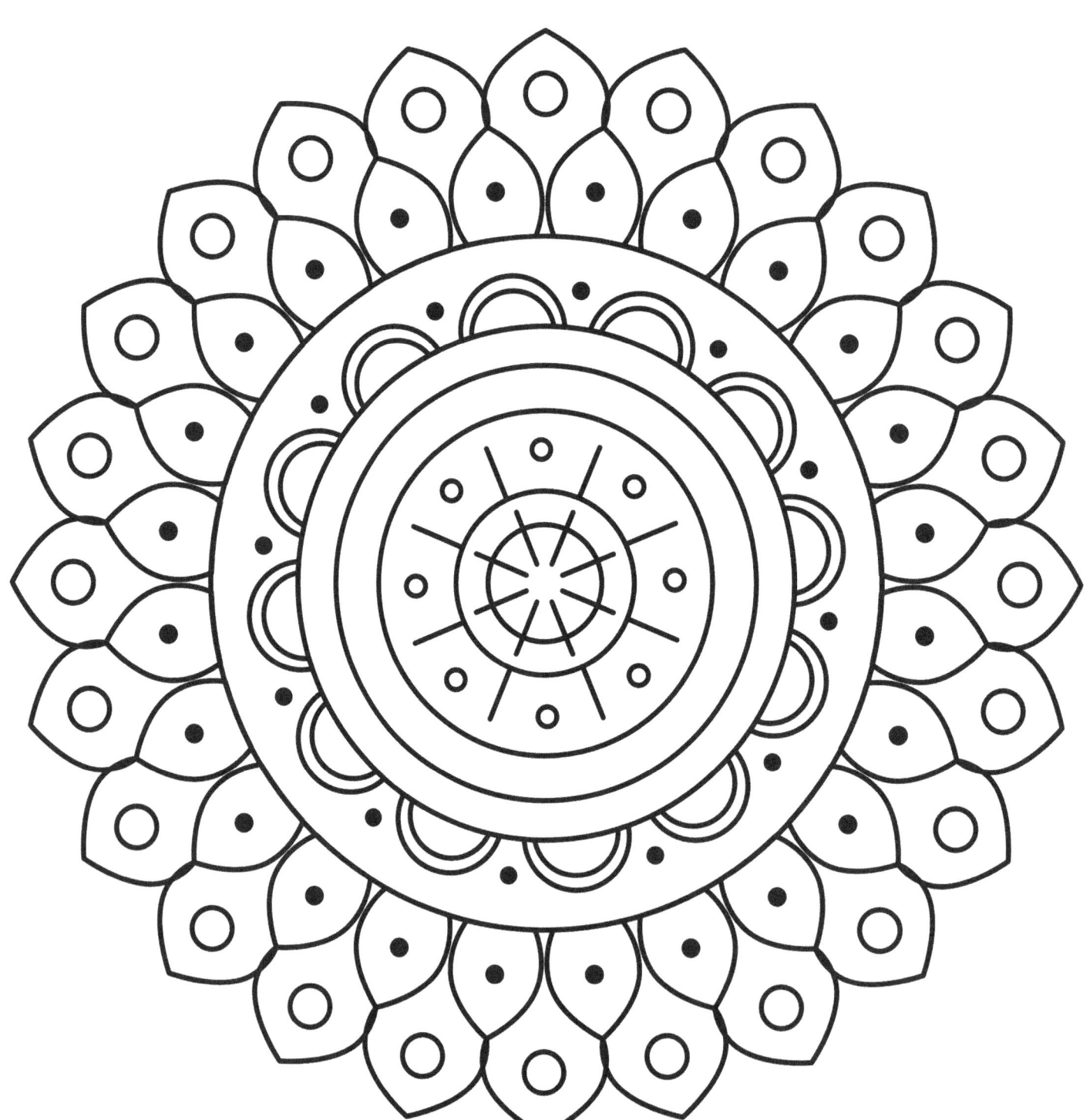

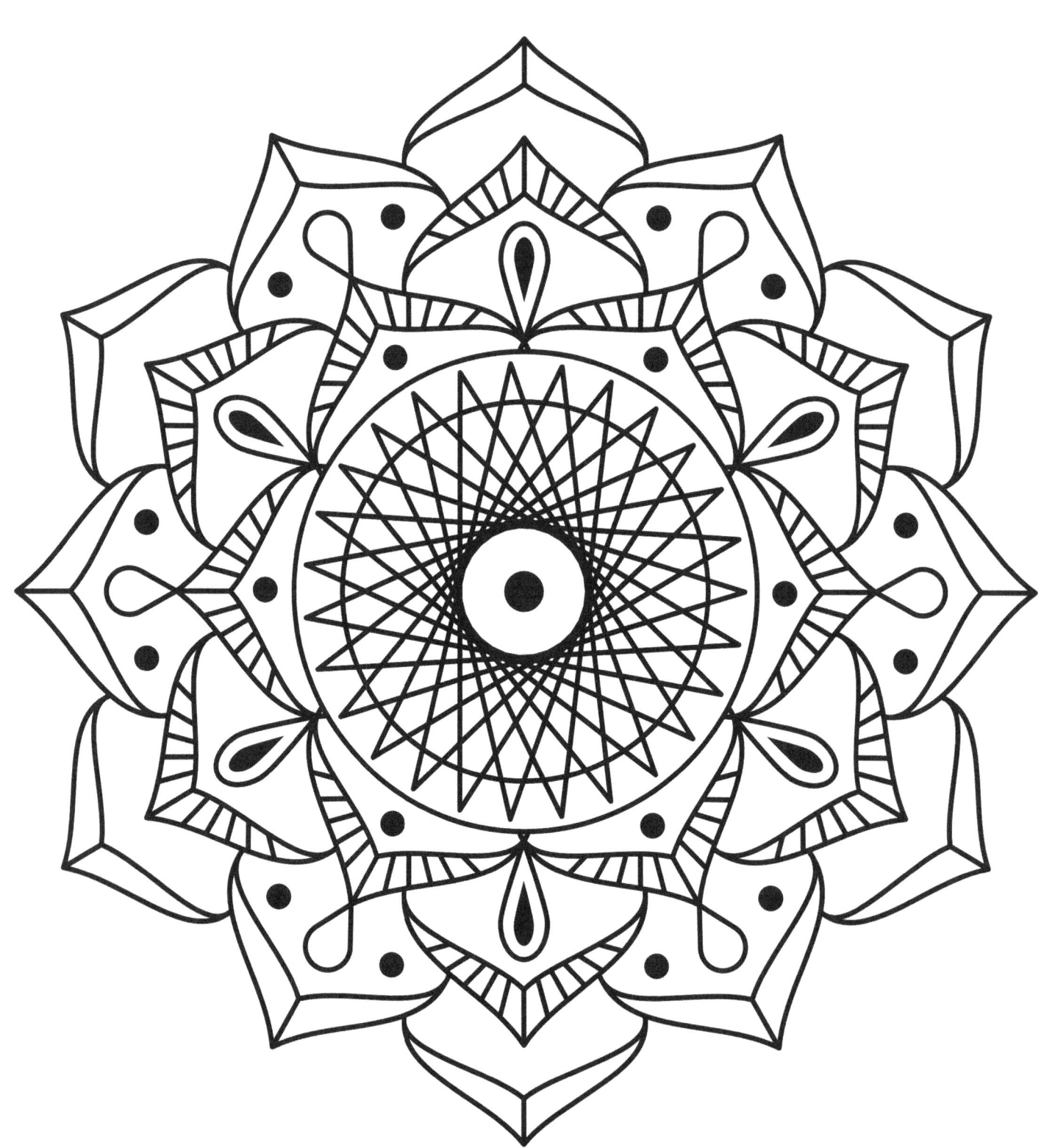

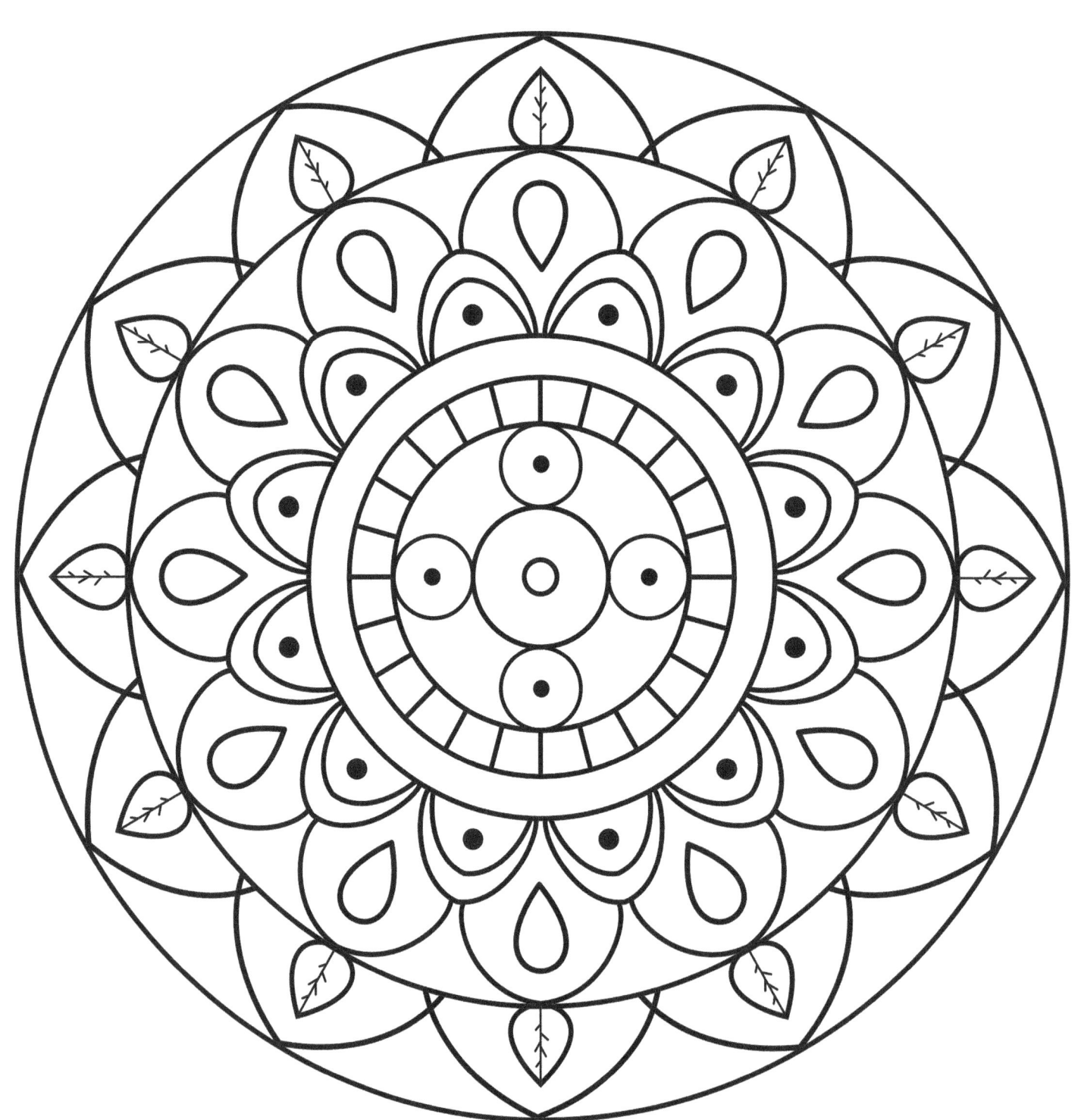

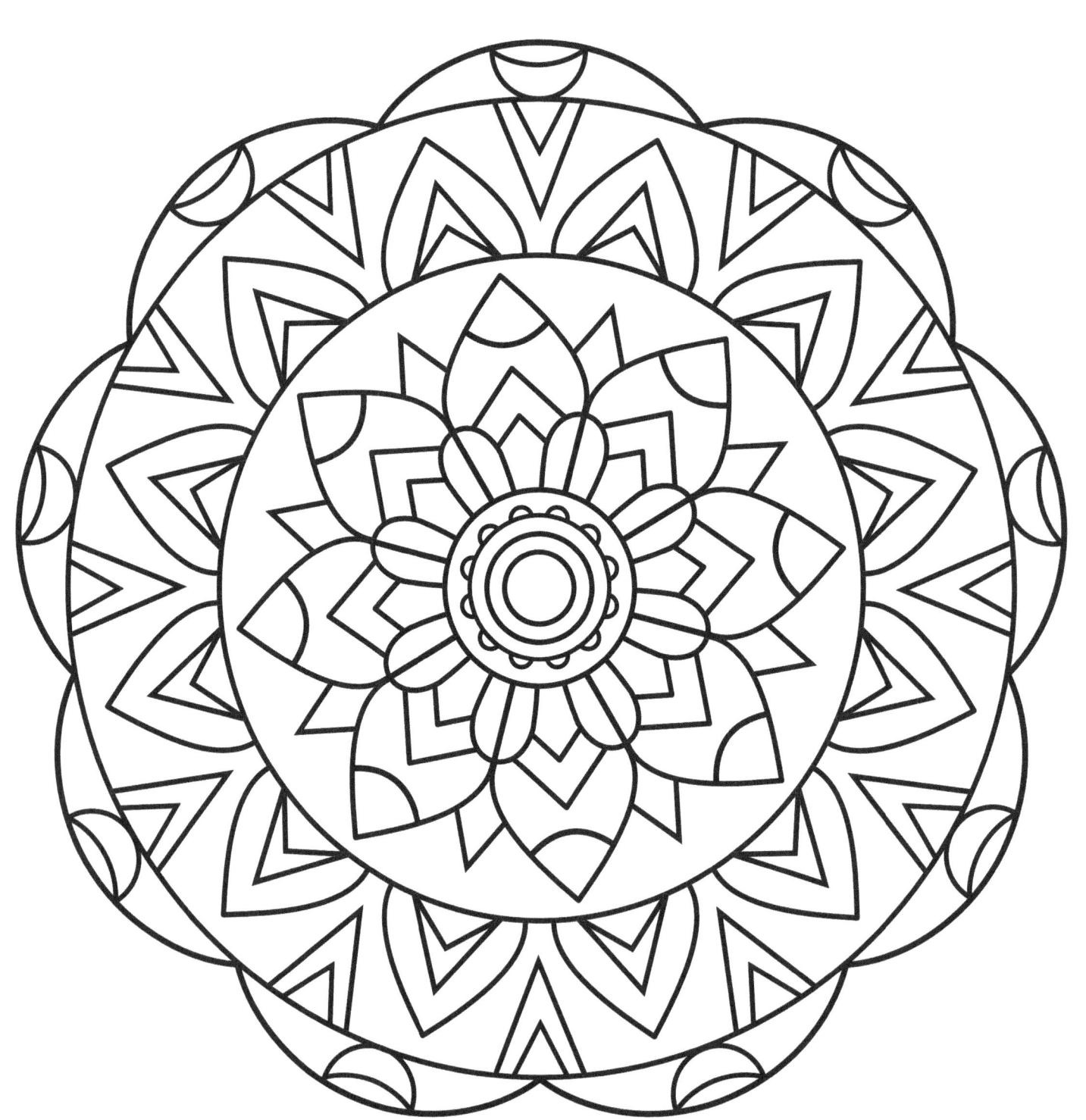

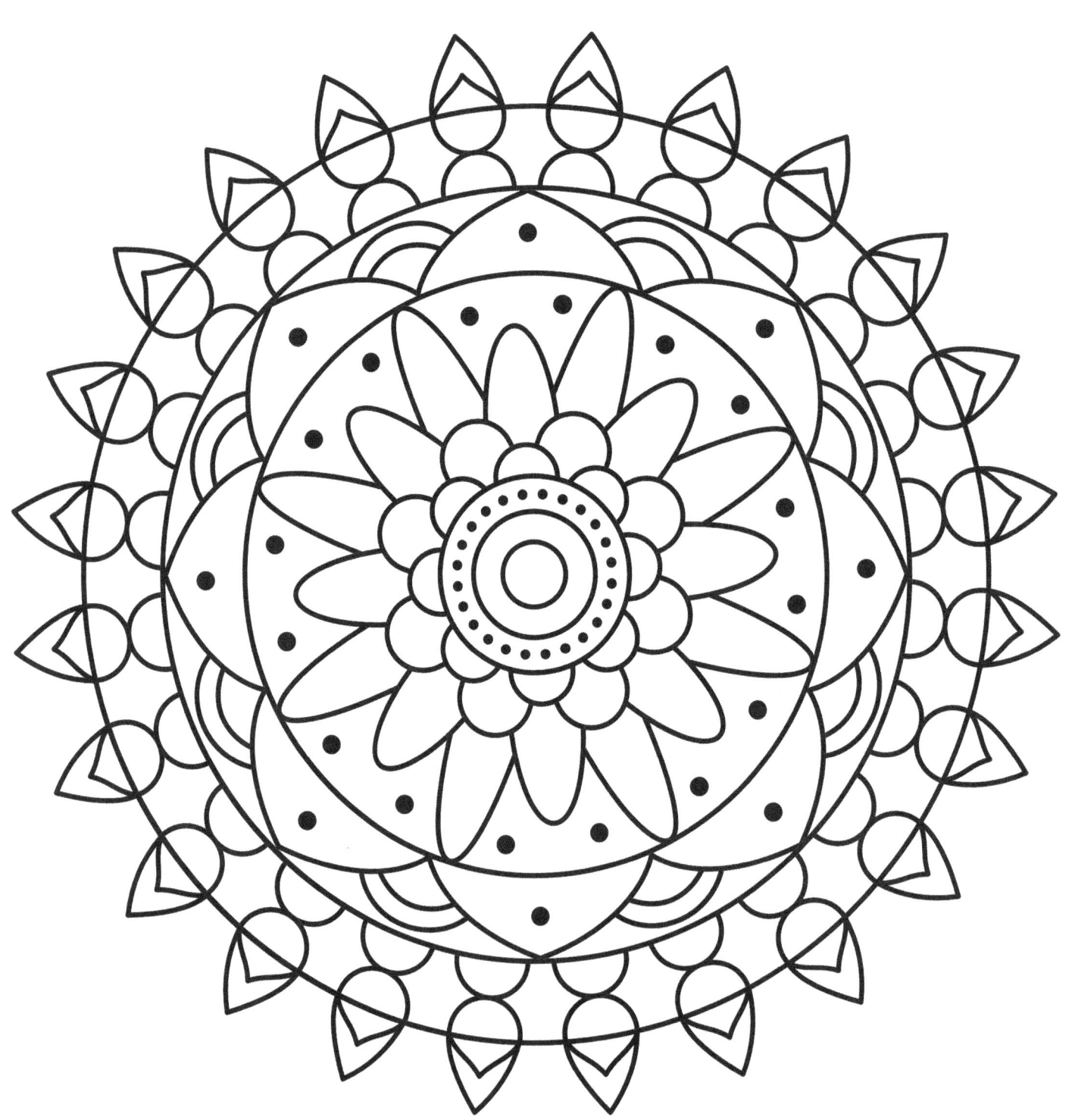

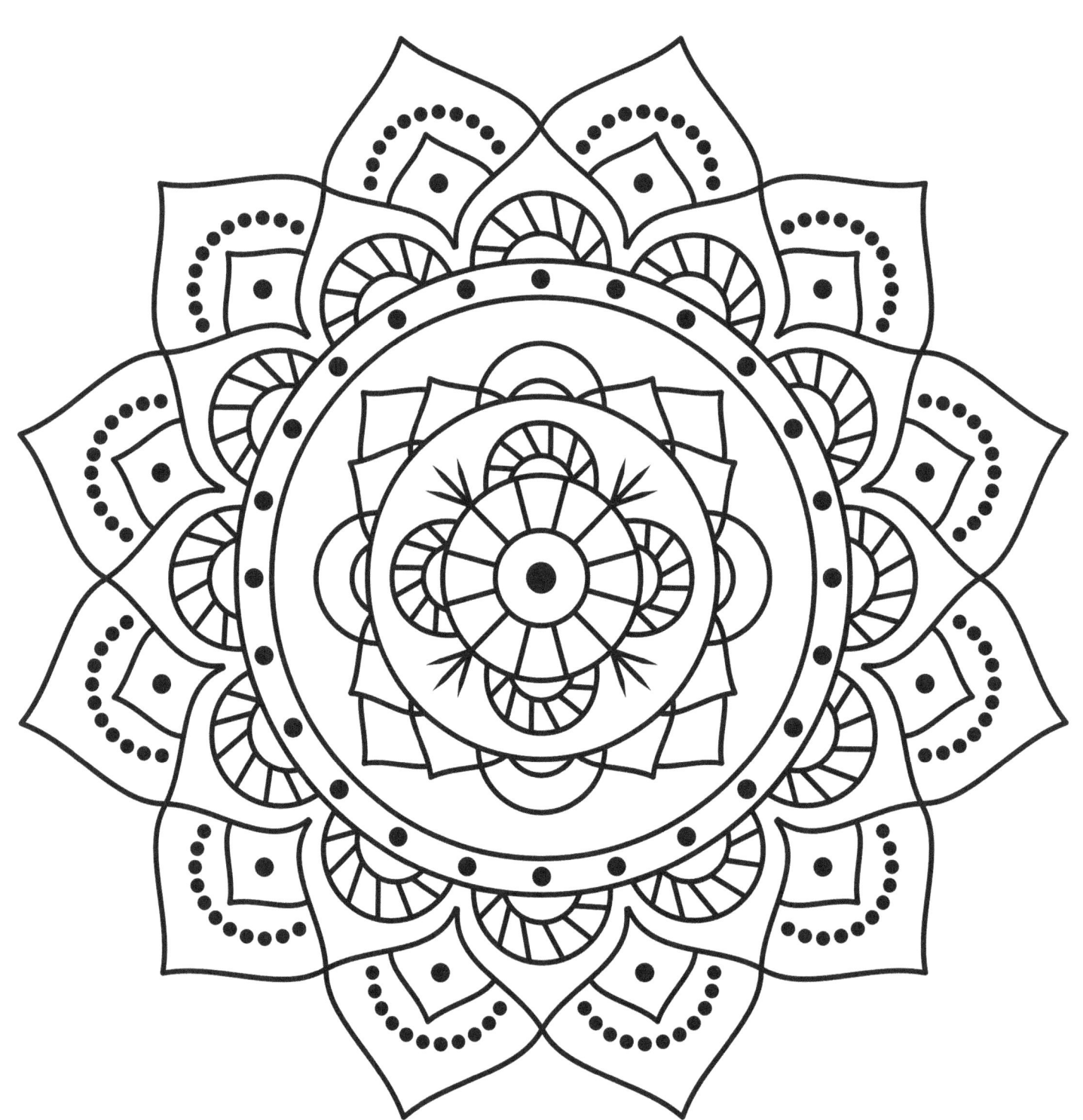

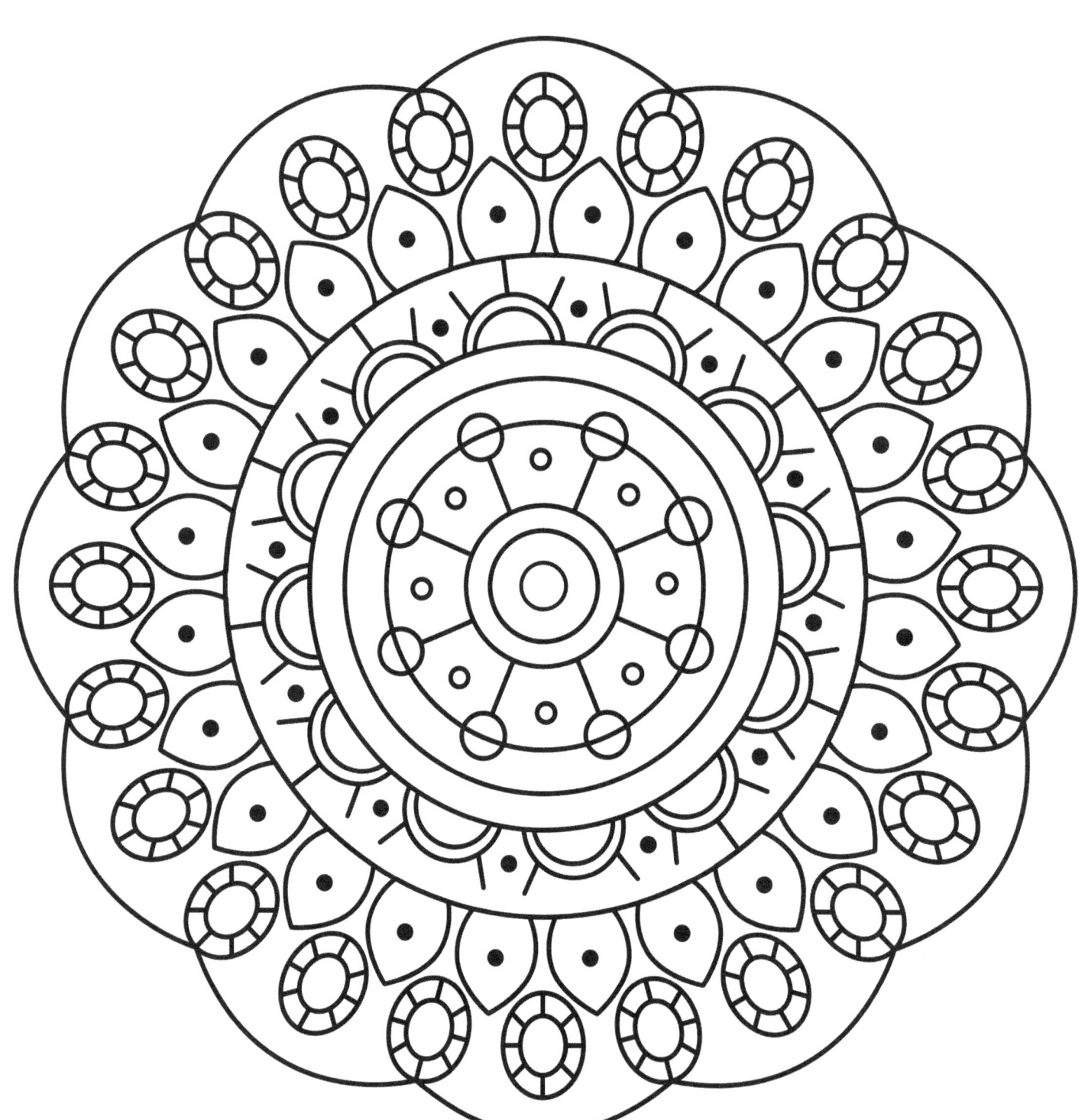

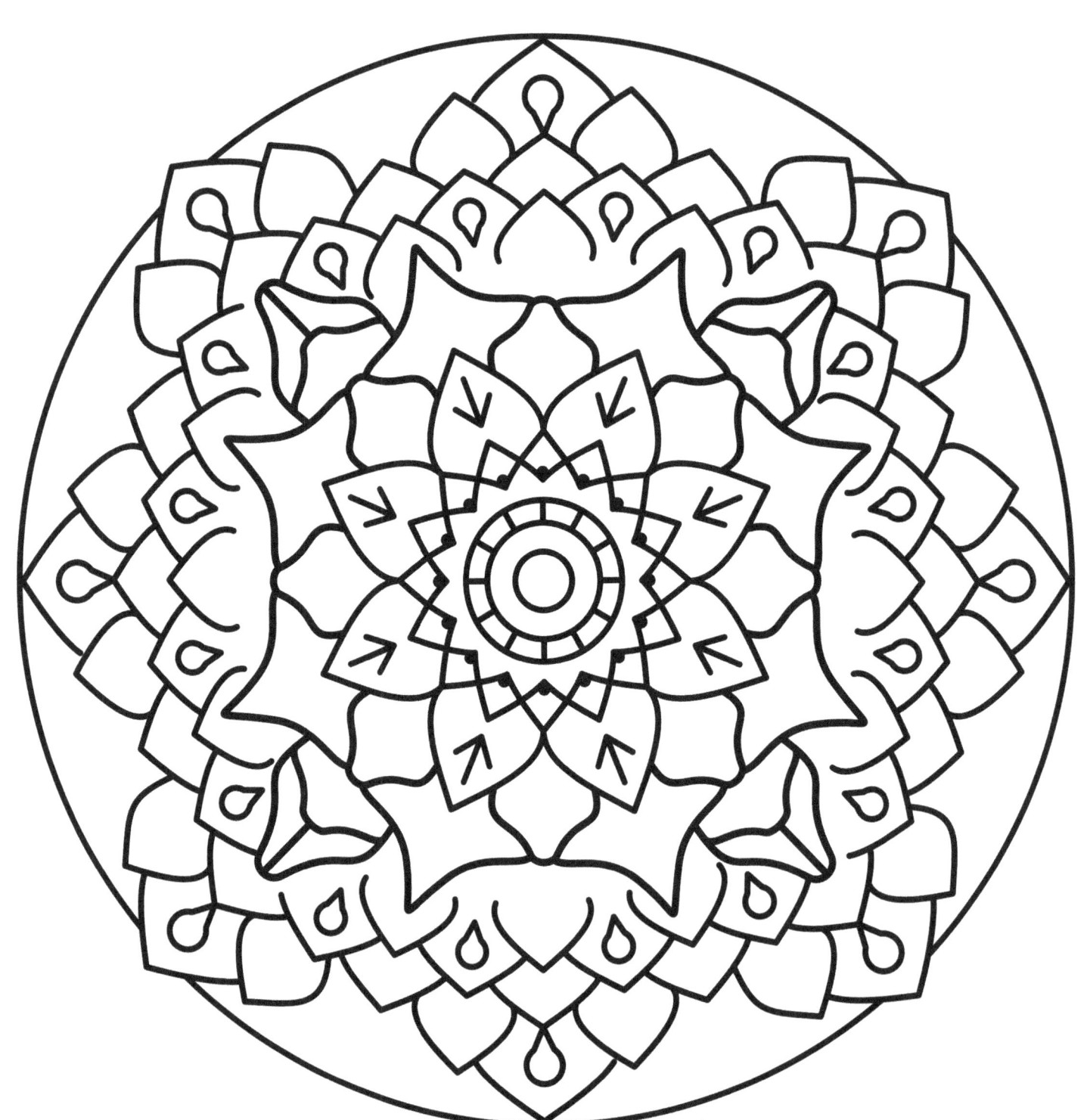

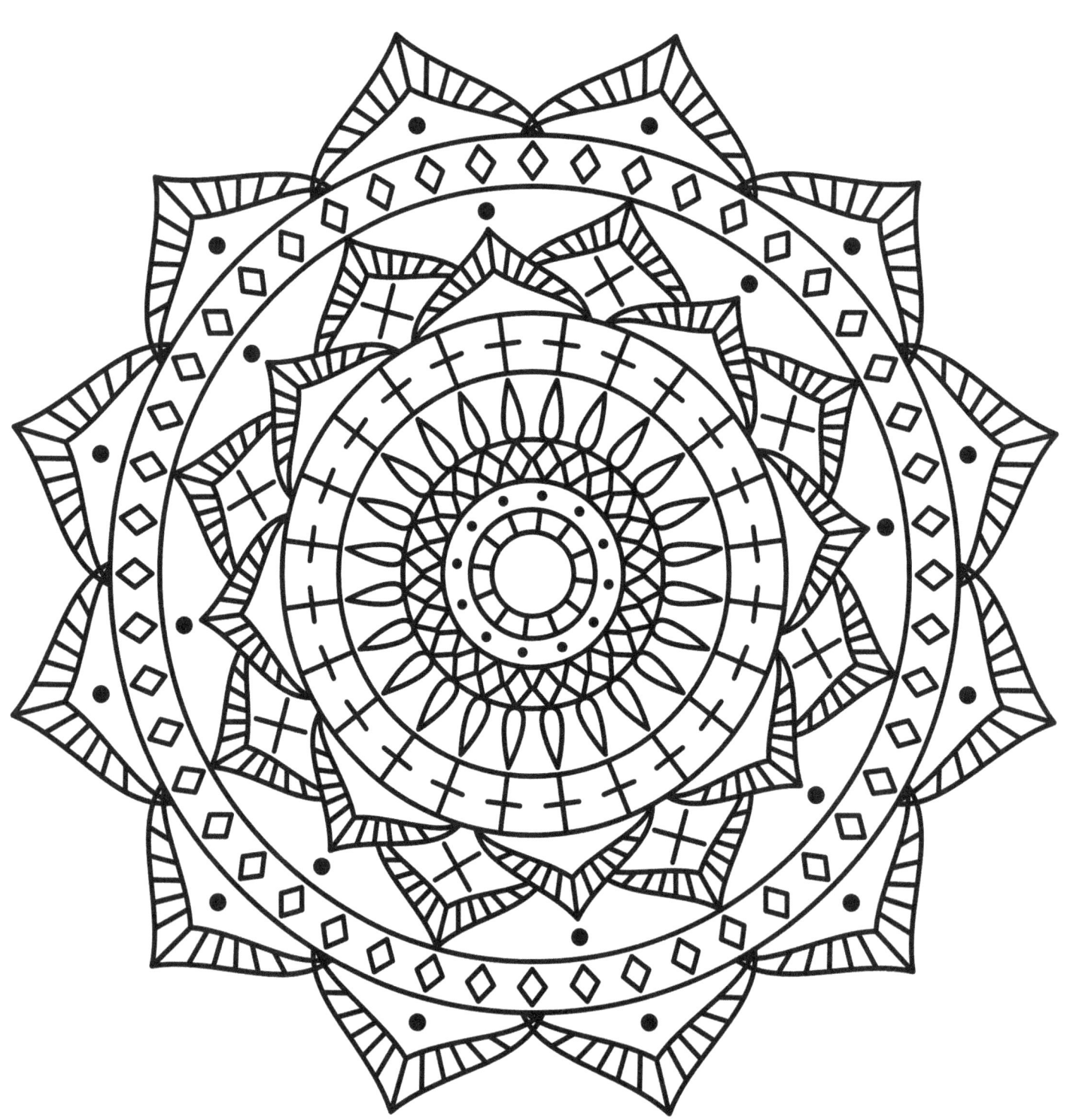

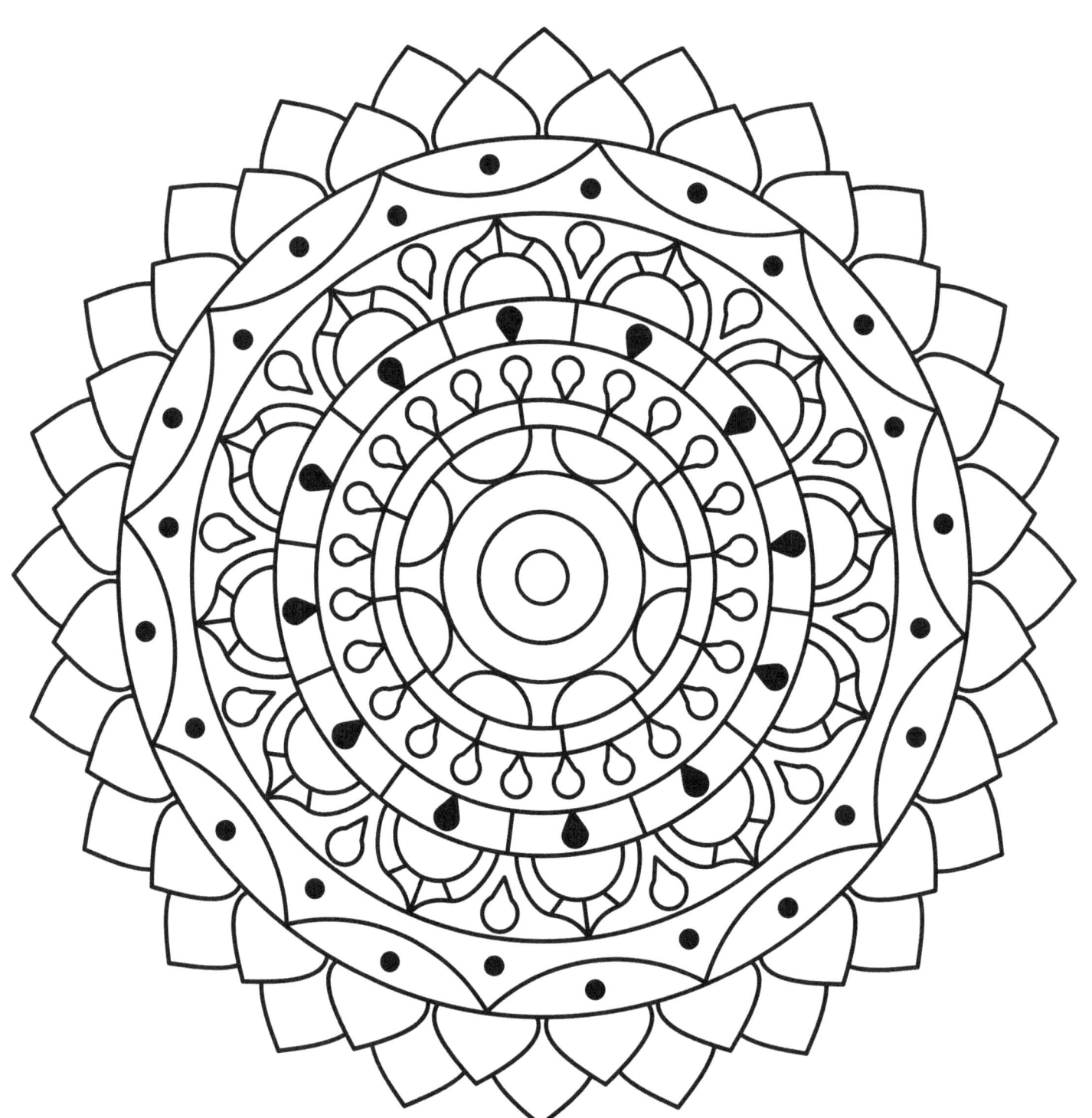

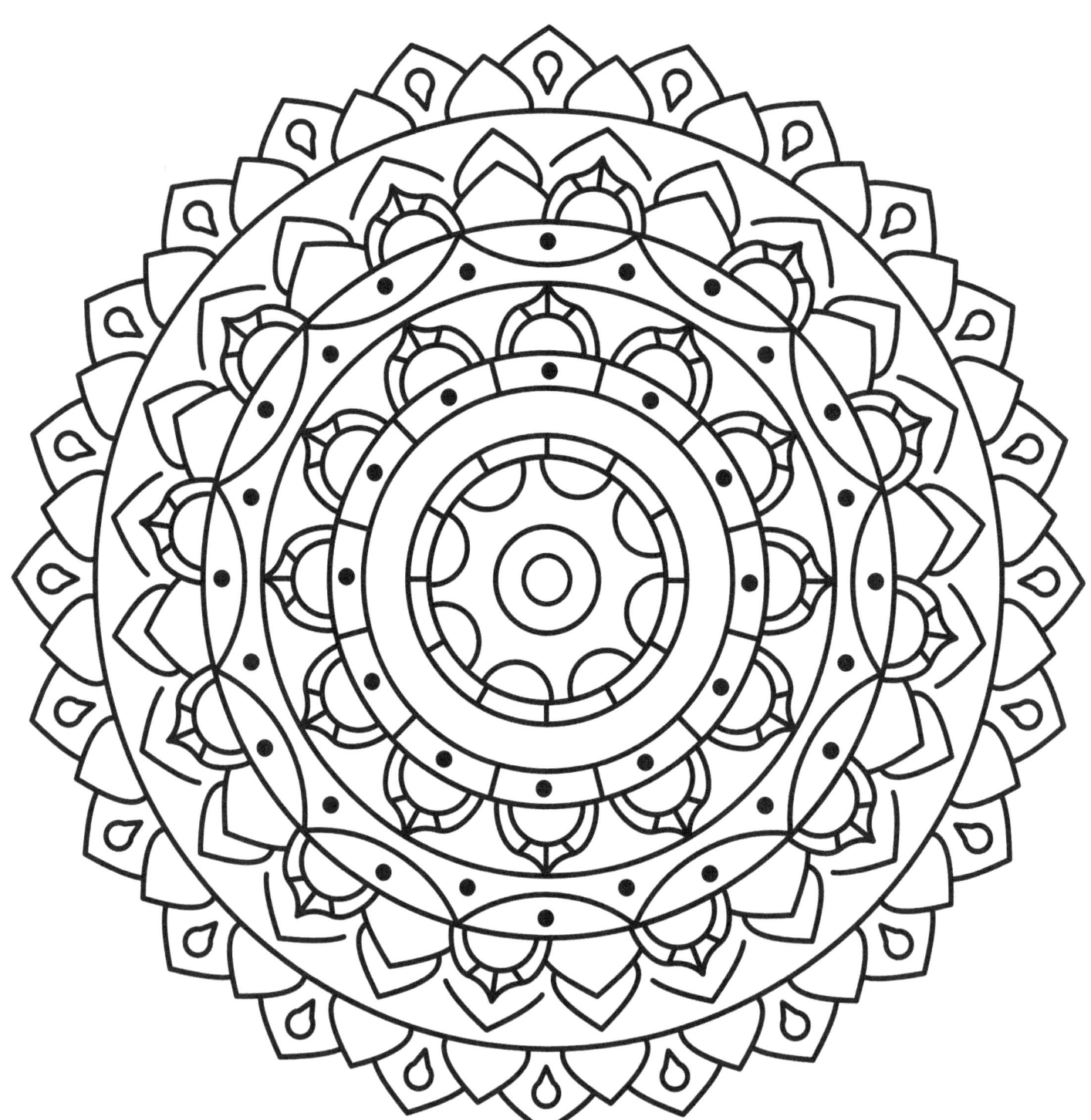

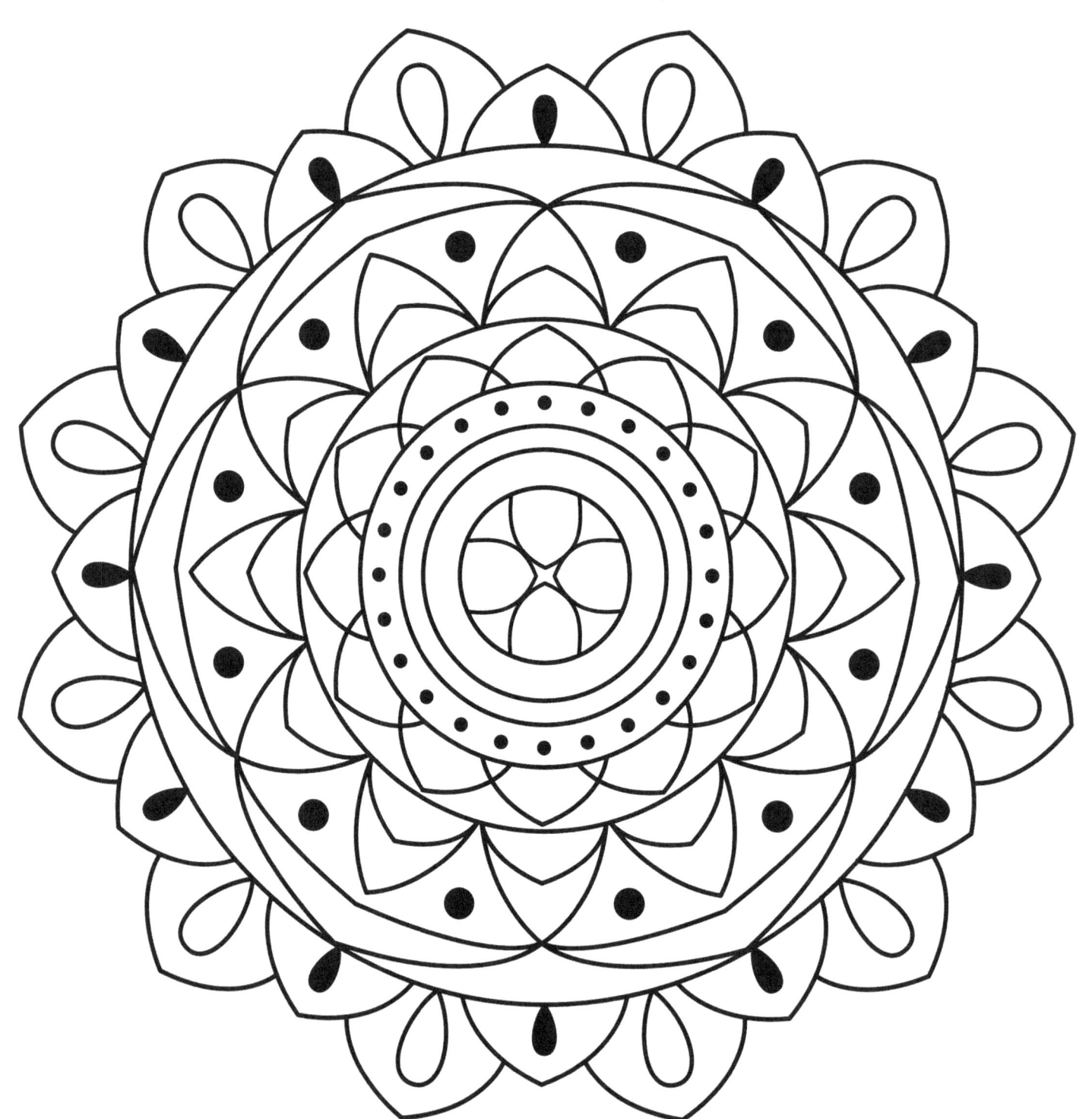

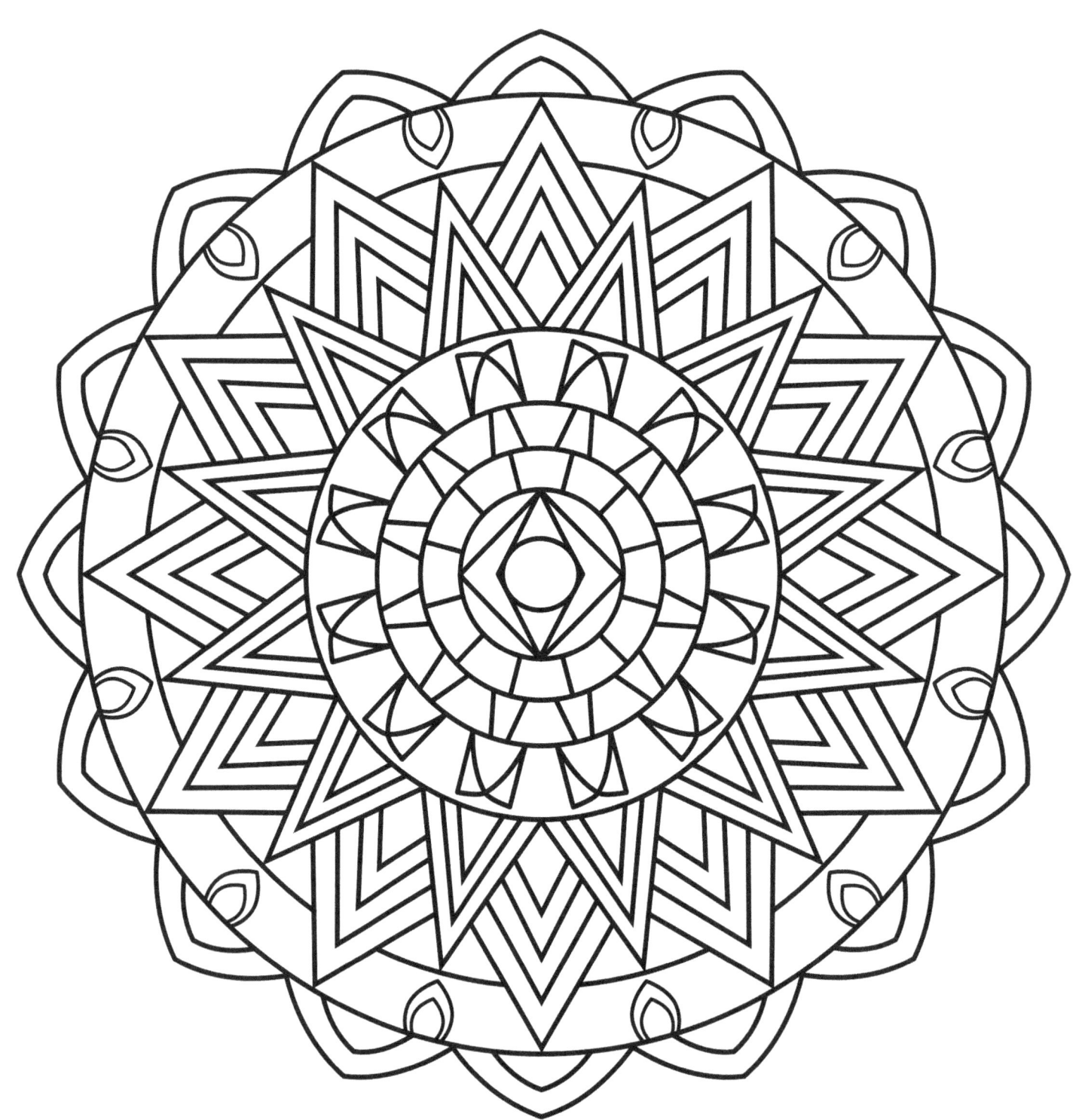

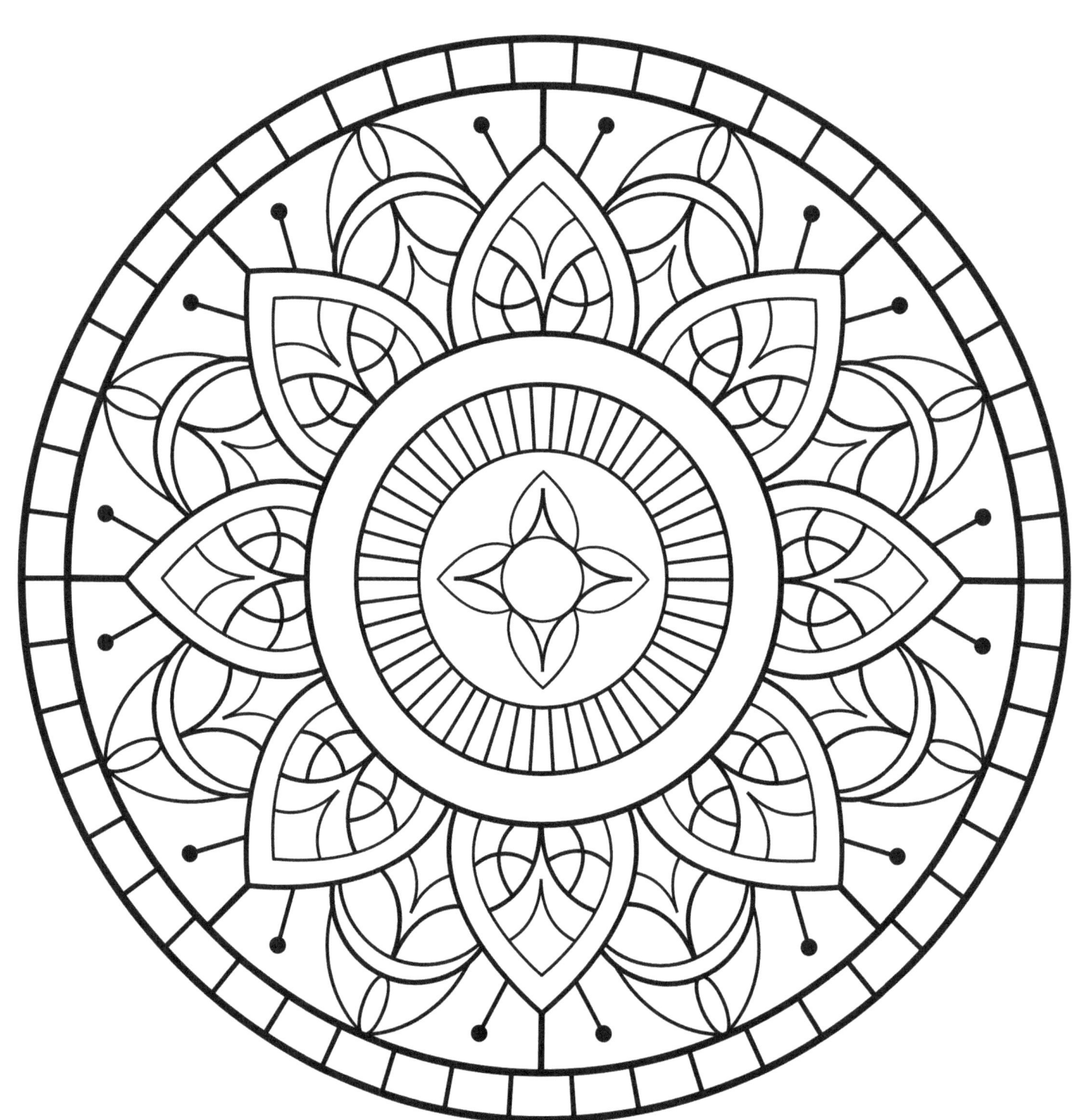

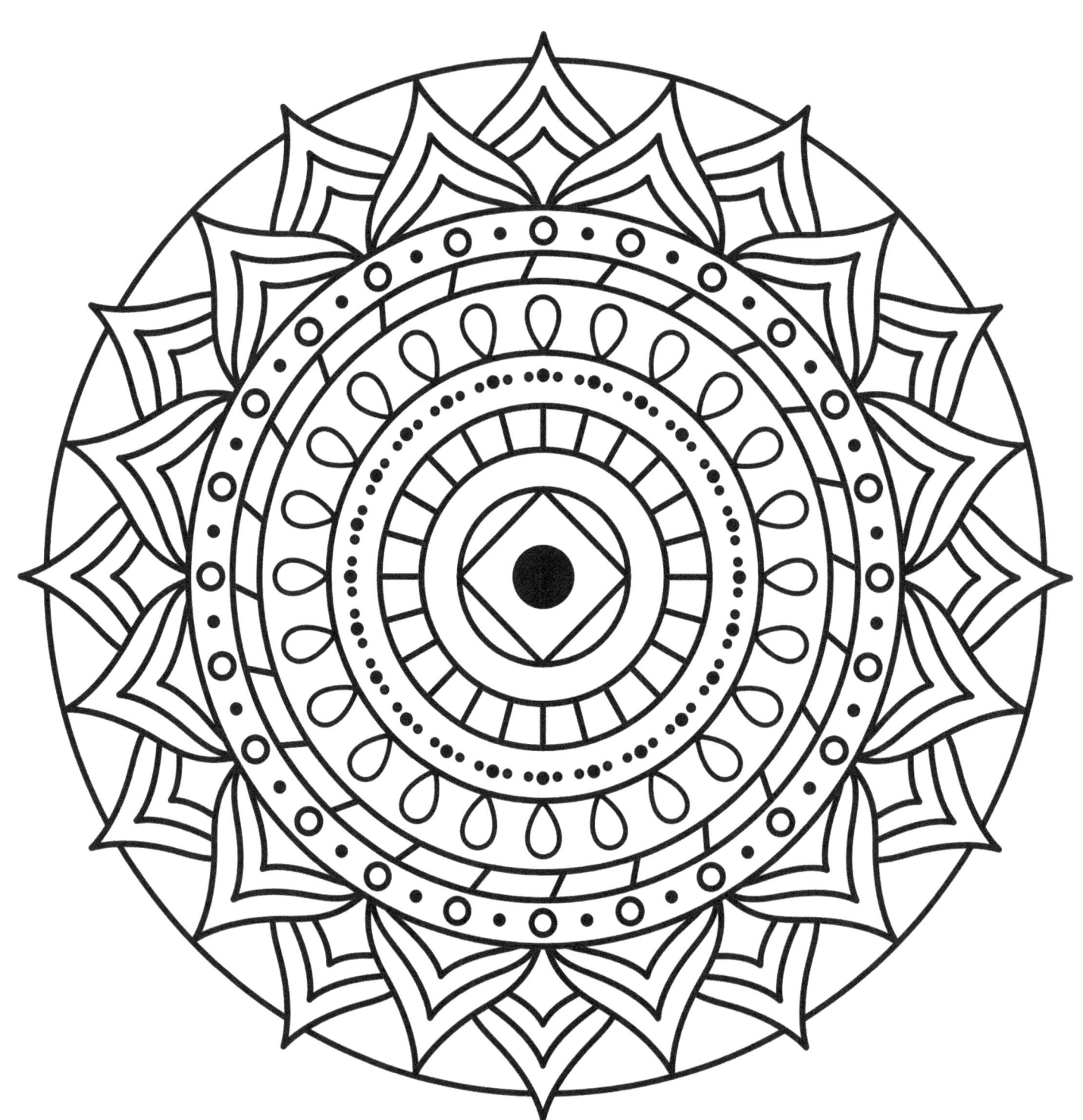

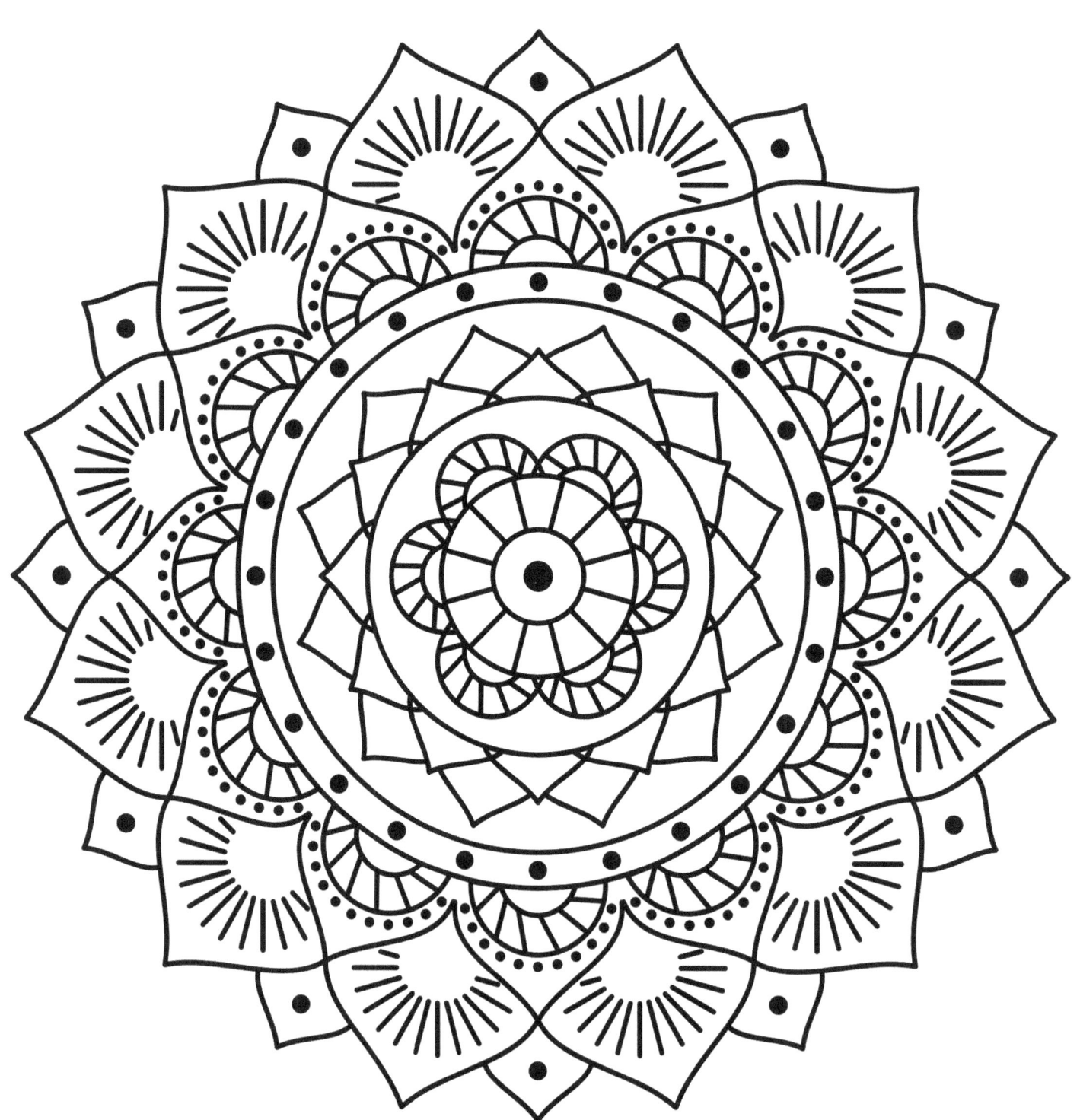

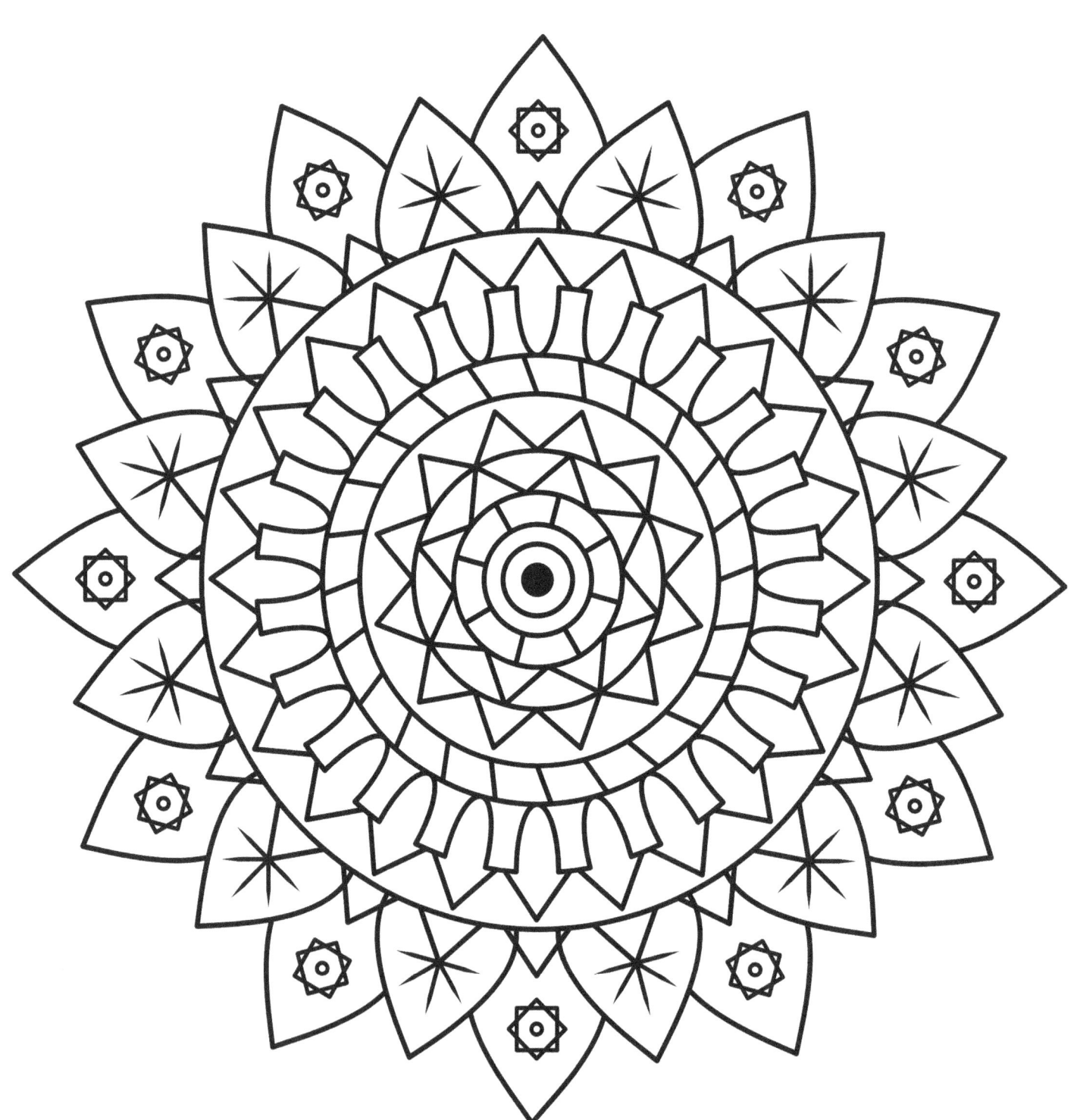

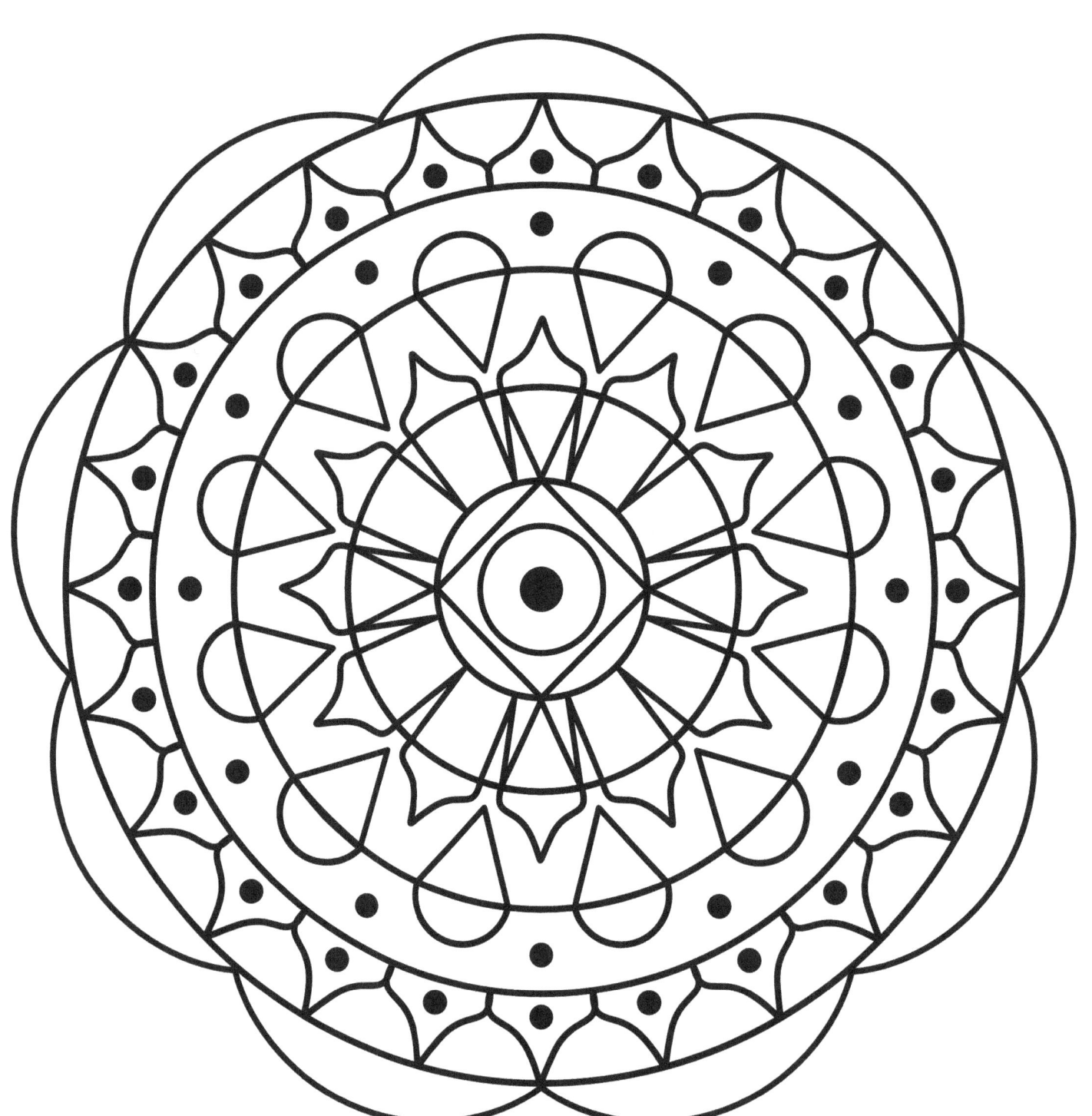

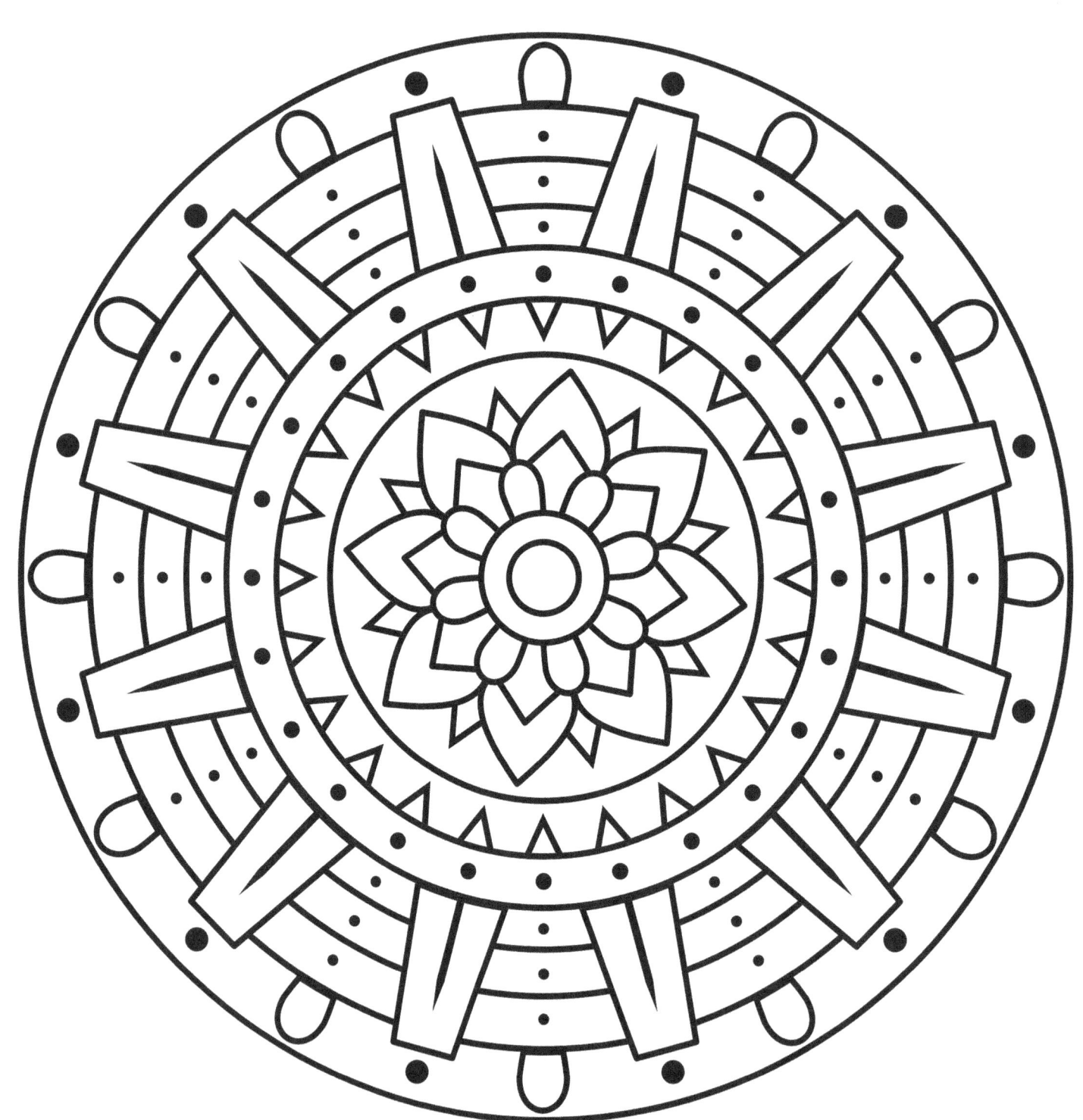

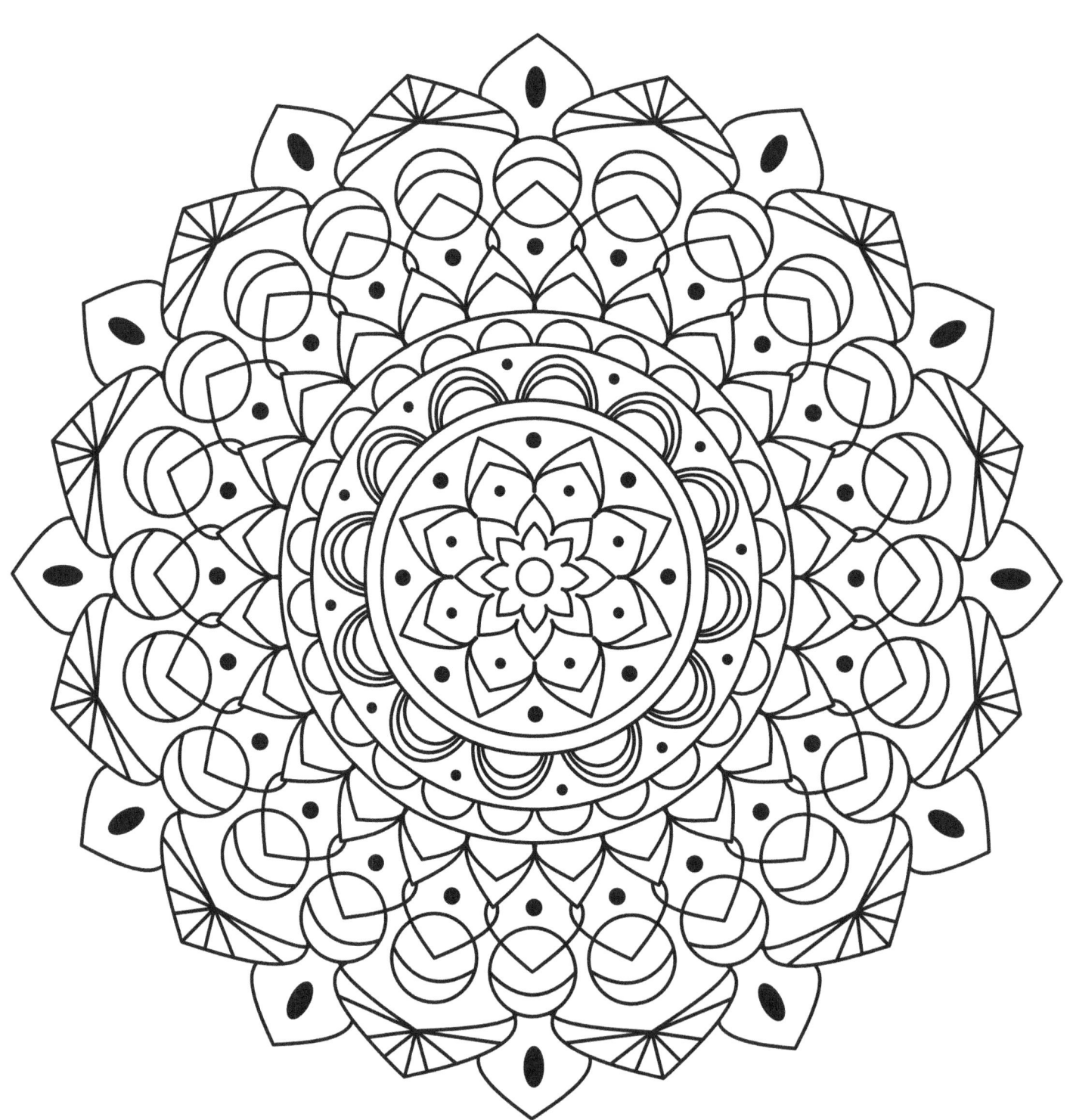

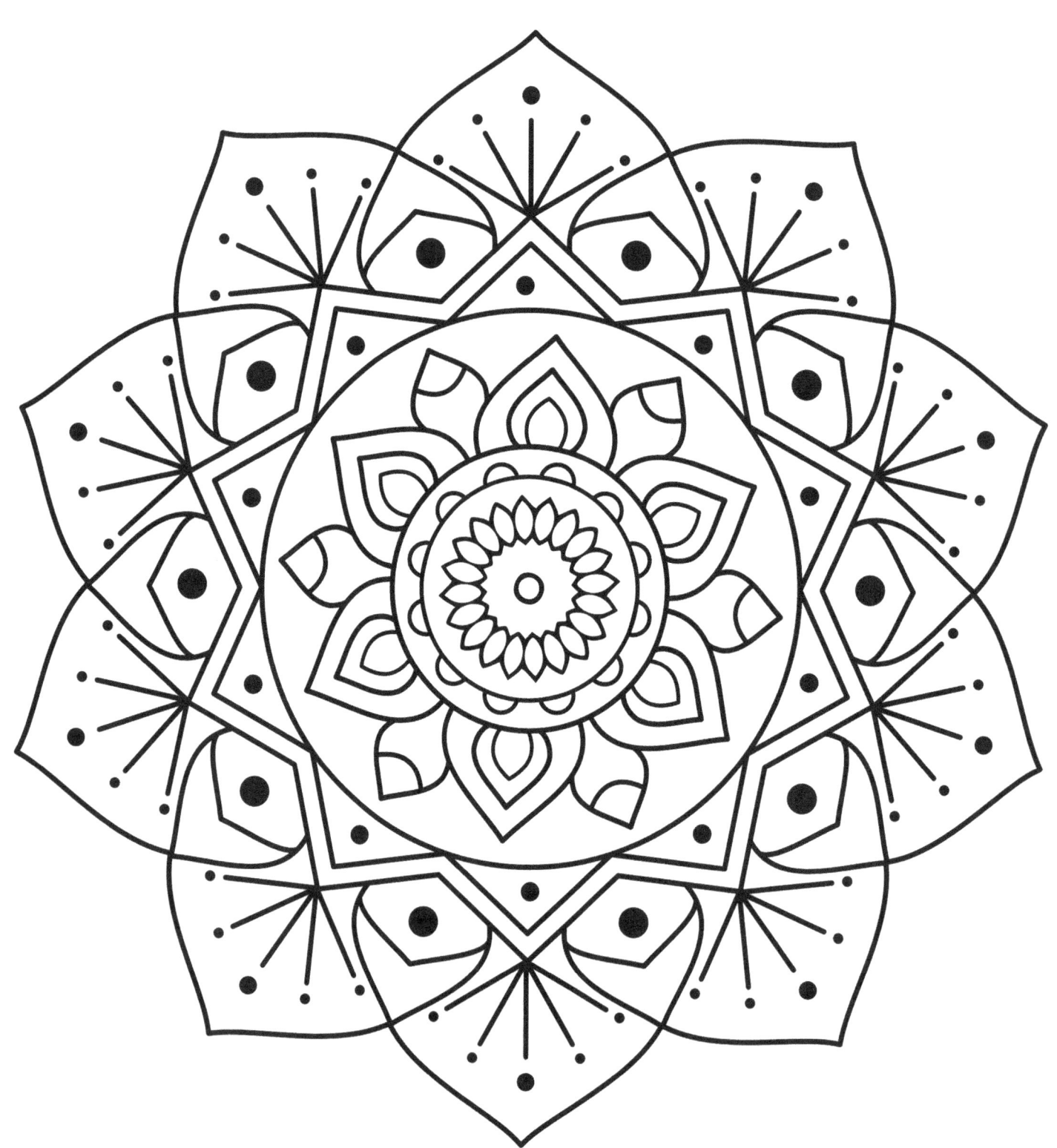

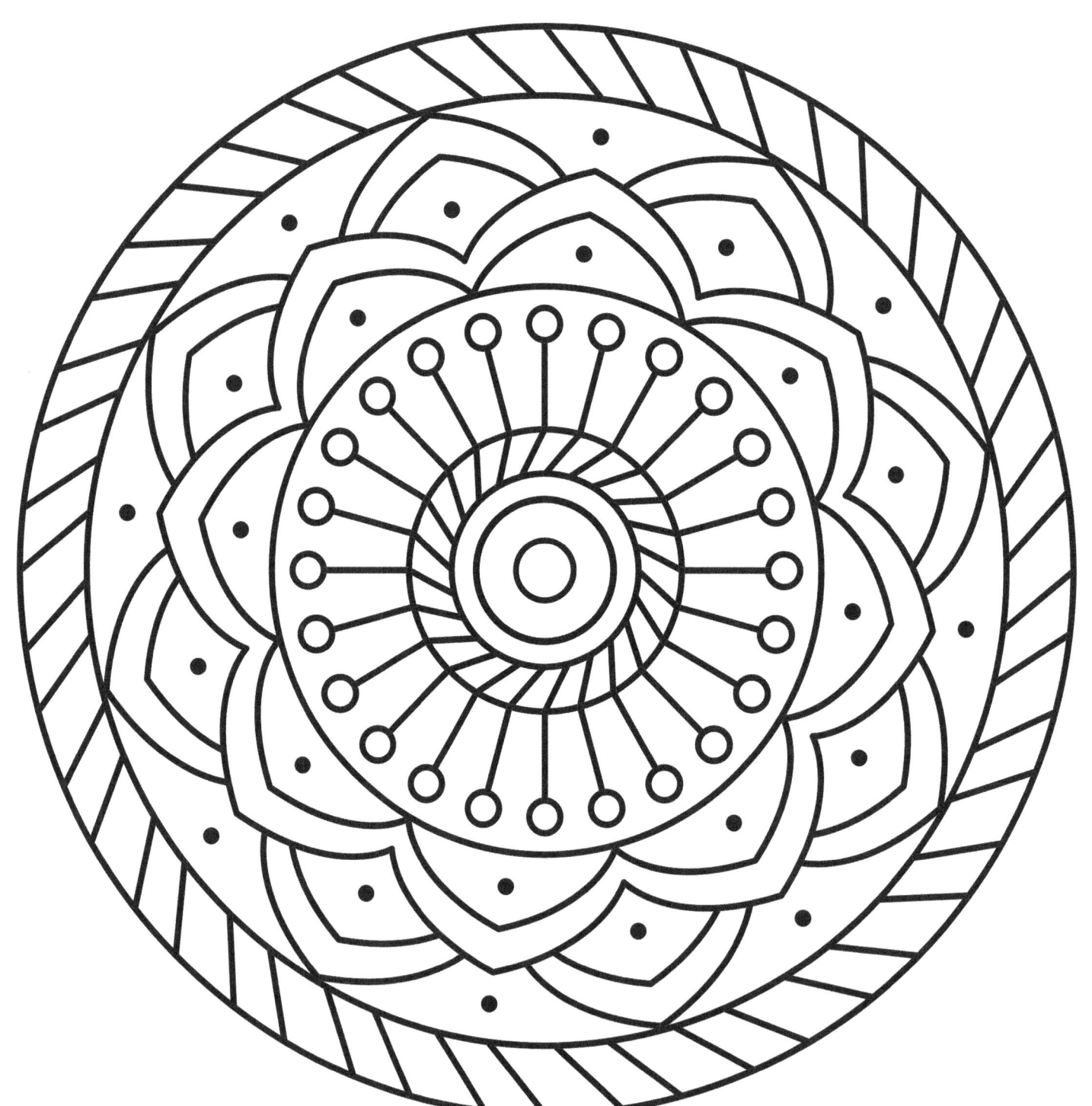

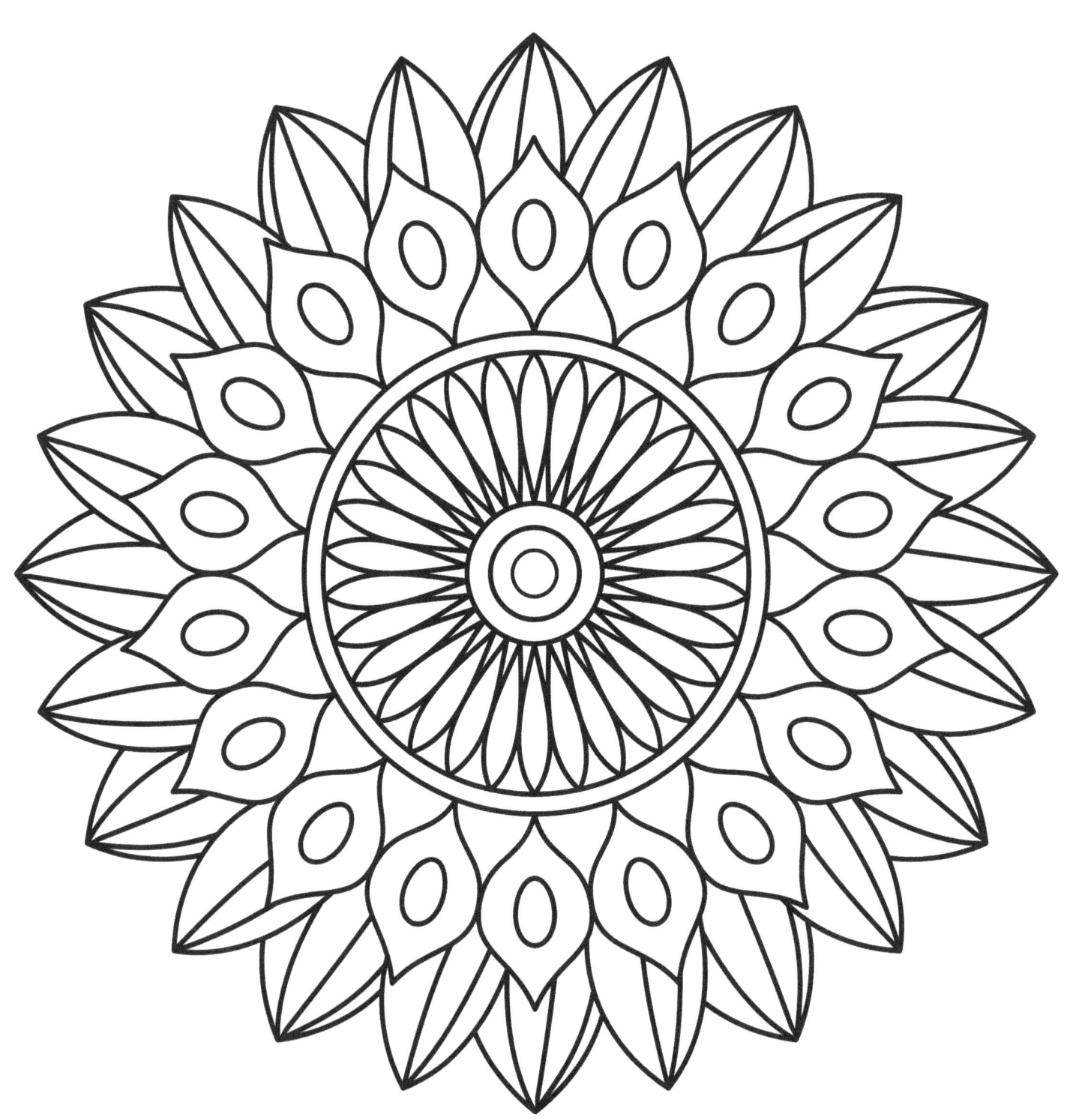

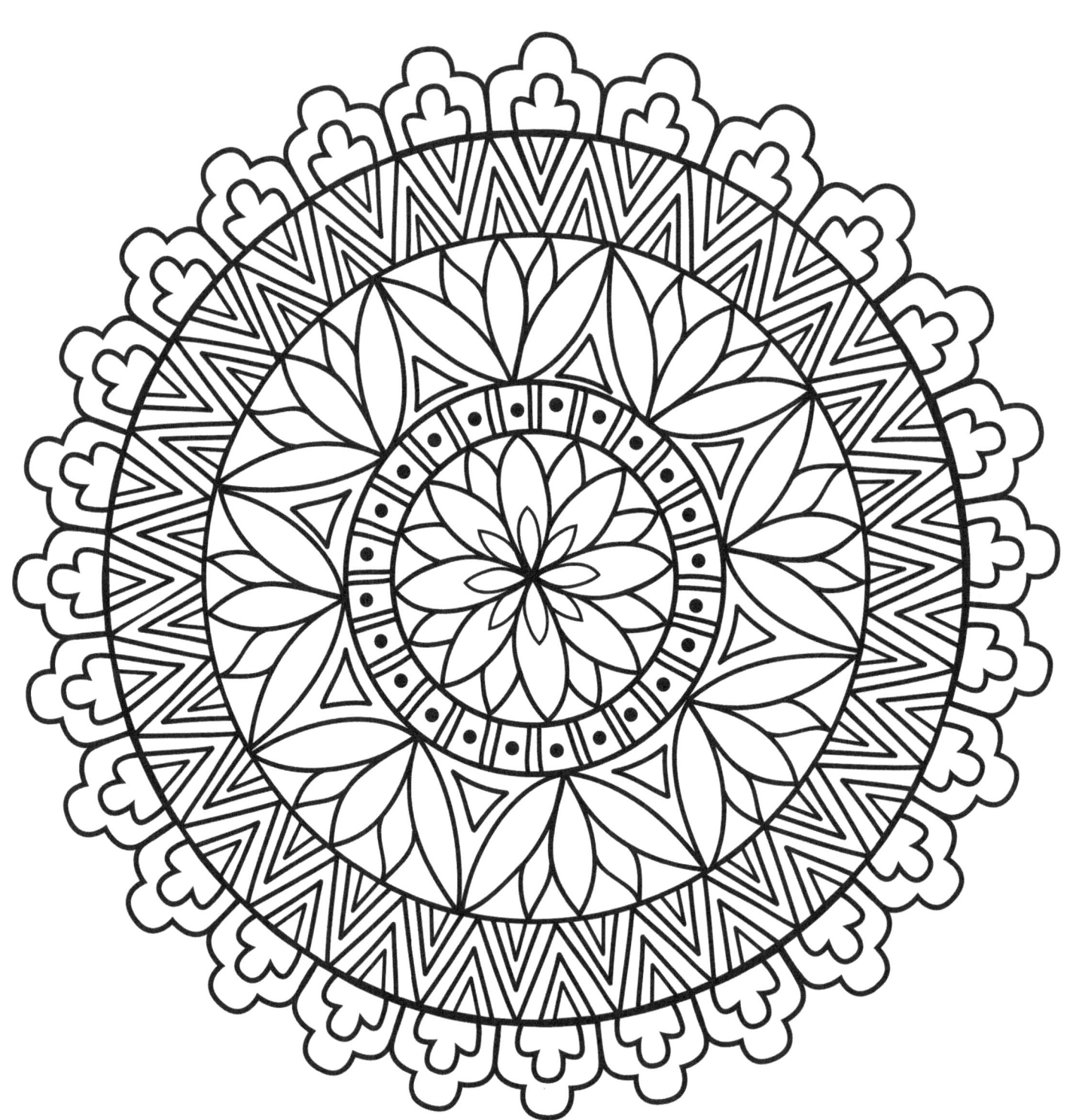

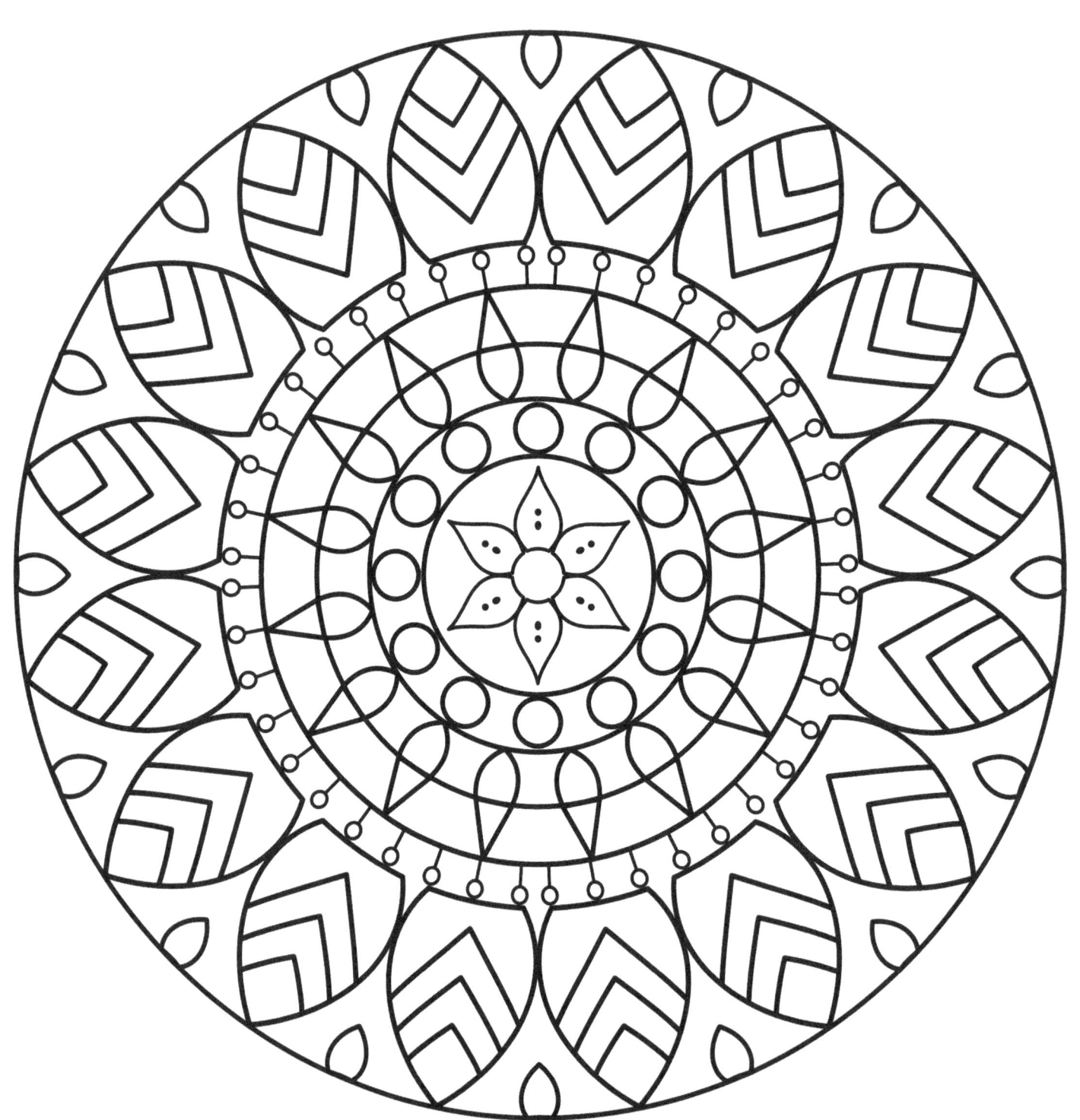

www.ingramcontent.com/pod-product-compliance
Lightning Source LLC
Chambersburg PA
CBHW080840220526

45467CB00008B/2348